The Scout
the Scout

Written by Steve Scholes

General Editor: Ron Jeffries

Designed and Illustrated by Anita Mason

 SBN 85165 148 8
Printed in Great Britain by Page Bros. (Norwich) Ltd., Norwich

First Edition May 1974
Fourth Edition May 1978
Second printing April 1979

The Scout Association
Baden-Powell House,
Queen's Gate, London SW7 5JS

Contents

Hi there!

wonder what kind of reader you are?

\re you a Cub Scout?

Perhaps you've just met your future Patrol Leader and he's ent you this book to help gain your **Link Badge** before you eave the Pack and join the Scout Troop?

Your Link Badge qualifies you for all but one of the require- nents of **The Scout Badge**, so it's worth having!

Your Scout Leader will help you to pass the one extra test.

Or are you quite new to Scouting?

Scouting is the biggest Movement for boys in the whole world, and you are joining a **family** where you'll have brothers wherever you move to.

It's great to meet you!

The Scout Badge

Knowledge of the Scout Movement
Show a general knowledge of the Scout Movement and the development of world-wide Scouting.

Robert Stephenson Smyth Baden-Powell was born in London on the 22nd. February, 1857.

His father, who died when Stephe was aged 3, was a clergyman and his mother was the daughter of an Admiral.

He was a very lively member of his family, skilful at drawing and sketching — in fact he could use each hand equally well! — and was very good at imitating bird and animal calls.

He went to school at Tunbridge Wells in Kent and from there went to Charterhouse on a scholarship. He was never very high up in his class, but in some of his outside interests—rifle shooting and amateur theatricals—he was outstanding.

When he wanted to be alone Stephe used to 'escape' to **The Copse**—a woodland wilderness near to the school. There he imagined himself to be a hunter or an Indian scout. He trapped animals and learned to cook them—and also learned how to avoid 'capture' by his teachers, as The Copse was out-of-bounds!

When he left school he sat an examination to enter the Army, passing so well that he was exempted from Sandhurst training and given a Commission in the 13th. Hussars.

His Army career took him to India, Afghanistan, Africa and other countries.

In 1888 B.-P. fought Chief Dinizulu—a Zulu chief—and captured him and his long necklace which consisted of hundreds of beads.

These beads were later used for the Scouter's **Wood Badge**, which is awarded to all Leaders who complete their adult leadership training.

Ask your Scout Leader to show you his Wood Badge if he has gained it yet.

Nowadays the beads are replicas but some original ones are still in circulation.

In the Army B.-P. spent much time trying to make the men's lives more interesting. He divided his men up into small units each under an Officer and those who successfully completed their training were awarded a badge in the form of an arrowhead. He wrote a book about it called *Aids to Scouting.*

In 1899 B.-P. successfully defended the town of Mafeking in the Transvaal for seven months against an attacking force of 9,000 men with only 1,000 men under him.

Ask your Patrol Leader to tell you the story. He can find details in *Scouting for Boys* or *The Scout Handbook.*

The Boers, against whom he was fighting, had all sorts of tricks played against them to make them think that the defences of Mafeking were stronger than they really were—dummy mines, searchlights (there was only one, made from a biscuit tin, that was moved about) and so on.

B.-P. returned to England a national hero and in 1903 became Inspector General of Cavalry, the highest position for a cavalry man.

He retired from the Army in 1907 with the rank of Lieutenant-General, free at last to put into practice the idea that had been forming in his mind: a scheme for giving more variety in the training of boys in good citizenship. **Scouting really began at . . . .** **Brownsea Island**

In 1907 B.-P. brought together a group of boys from all kinds of backgrounds and they camped at Brownsea Island off the Dorset coast. He wanted to re-write *Aids to Scouting* as a book for boys, and he hoped through this camp to find out if his ideas would work.

Twenty-one boys were divided into four Patrols, **Curlews, Ravens, Wolves** and **Bulls,** and from 31st. July to 9th. August, 1907 the boys learned all about camping, hiking, stalking, life-saving, boating and many more of the things that you will do as a Scout.

The camp was a huge success—it had proved that boys could be trusted to organise themselves and that when put *on their honour* they would do their very best. Following the camp B.-P. wrote his book *Scouting for Boys* (you can still buy a copy through Scout Shops Ltd.—your Patrol should have a copy) and thousands of boys bought it eagerly and started Patrols and Troops for themselves all over the country. **Scouting had started**!

Patrol Leader—how about discussing at your next Patrol Leaders' Council holding your next summer camp at Brownsea Island? See where Scouting started!

The Scouting Family

Cub Scouts (8-11)

Extension Scouts for boys with a handicap

Air Scouts

Scouts (11-16)

Sea Scouts

Venture Scouts (16-20)

Meet the Chiefs!

On 7th. August, 1920 as B.-P. was about to close the Ist. International Jamboree held at Olympia, London, a young Scout declared, *'We, the Scouts of the World, salute you, Sir Robert Baden-Powell, Chief Scout of the World'*—and so by the acclamation of the boys themselves B.-P. became the only ever **Chief Scout of the World.**

He received many other honours—King George V created him **Lord Baden-Powell of Gilwell** and he was later awarded the rare and distinguished **Order of Merit.**

B.-P. died on 8th. January, 1941 and is buried in Kenya.

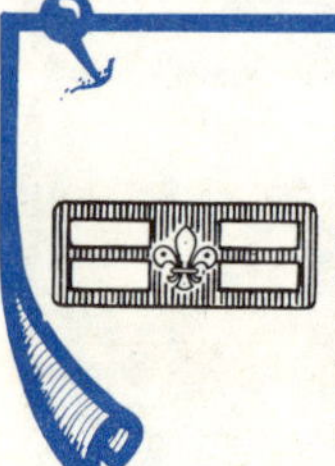

Patrol Leader—ask Skip if he'll book the film *Baden-Powell, Chief Scout of the World* **from the Scout Film Library. Details of this and other films can be obtained from the Public Relations Department, Baden-Powell House, Queen's Gate, London SW7 5JS. Arrange for your Patrol to meet the Founder.**

Lord Somers, a friend of B.-P., had the difficult task of leadership as Chief Scout during the war years (from 1941) until his death in 1944.

He was followed by **Lord Rowallan,** who was Chief Scout from 1945 to 1959, with the equally difficult task of experiment and development within Scouting to bring it up-to-date and revitalize it after the war years.

In 1959 he retired to become Governor of Tasmania and handed over the task of Chief Scout to **Lord Maclean,** who was largely responsible through his **Advance Party** for the changes that renamed Wolf Cubs as **Cub Scouts,** Boy Scouts as **Scouts**, and introduced **Venture Scouts**, along with the terrific new training programme that we all enjoy today. In 1972 Her Majesty The Queen invited him to become her Lord Chamberlain and so he resigned as **Chief Scout of the United Kingdom,** but continued to be **Chief Scout of the Commonwealth** until 1975.

Sir William Gladstone

1973 saw our present Chief, **Sir William Gladstone,** great grandson of the famous Prime Minister William Ewart Gladstone (1809-1898), become Chief Scout of the United Kingdom. You may be lucky enough to meet him.

The Chief lives with his family at Hawarden Castle in Clwyd, North Wales.

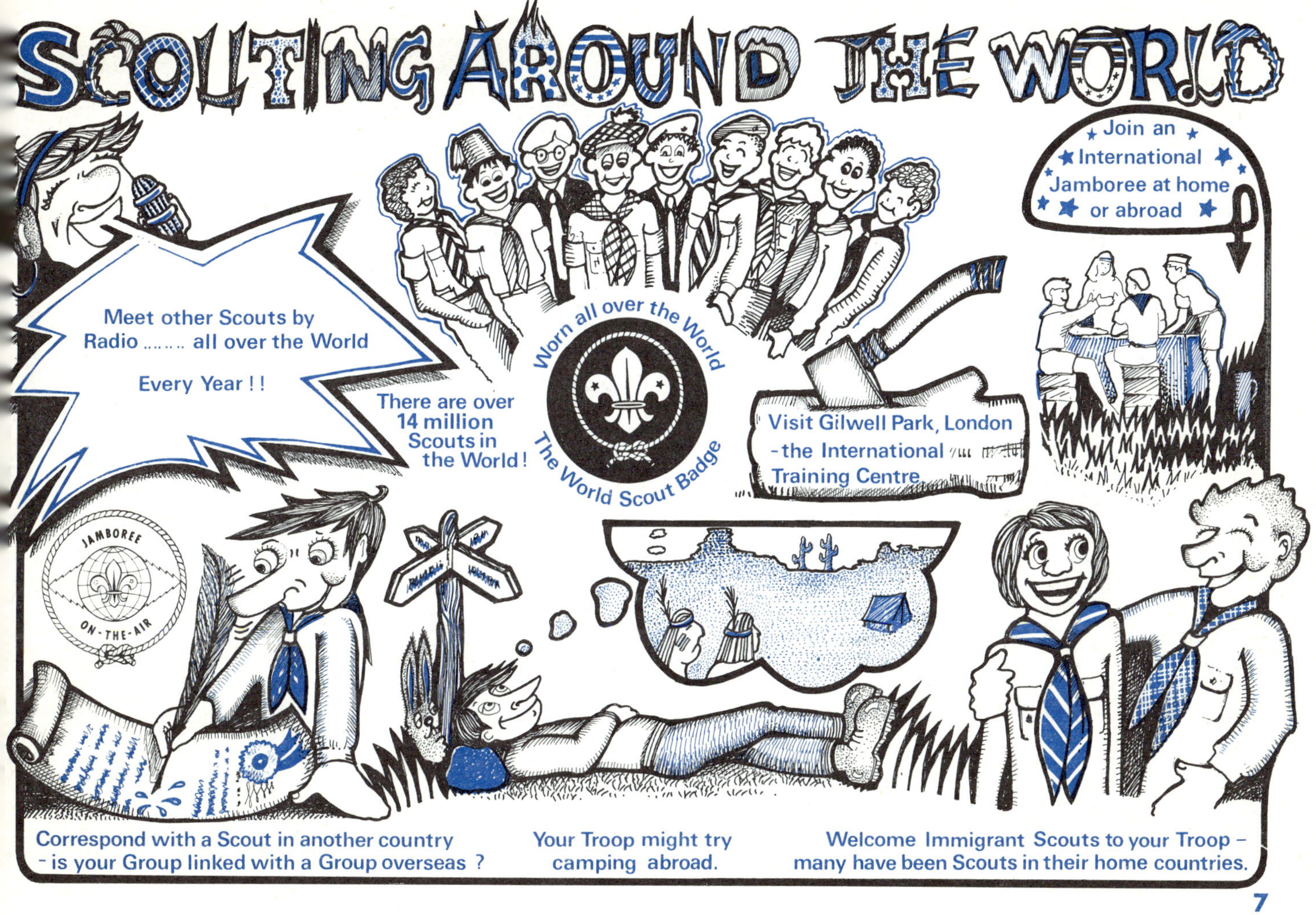
SCOUTING AROUND THE WORLD
Meet other Scouts by Radio .... all over the World
Every Year ! !
There are over 14 million Scouts in the World !
Worn all over the World
The World Scout Badge
Join an International Jamboree at home or abroad
Visit Gilwell Park, London - the International Training Centre
JAMBOREE ON-THE-AIR
Correspond with a Scout in another country - is your Group linked with a Group overseas ?
Your Troop might try camping abroad.
Welcome Immigrant Scouts to your Troop - many have been Scouts in their home countries.

Outdoor Activity
Take part in a Patrol or Troop activity out-of-doors.

Why not try to attempt all of these activities before this time next year?

Build a tree platform and sleep in it – be sure to tie yourself securely in!!

Go on a night hike or cycle ride. Try travelling using the stars as direction finders. Check lights and brakes.

Go canoeing. How about a Patrol afternoon fishing contest? Have a swimming session at your local open-air pool or beach, and use the 'Buddy System' when you do.

Patrol Leader—treat the new member of your Patrol as a special guest—it's easy for him to feel shy or embarrassed if he doesn't know anyone.

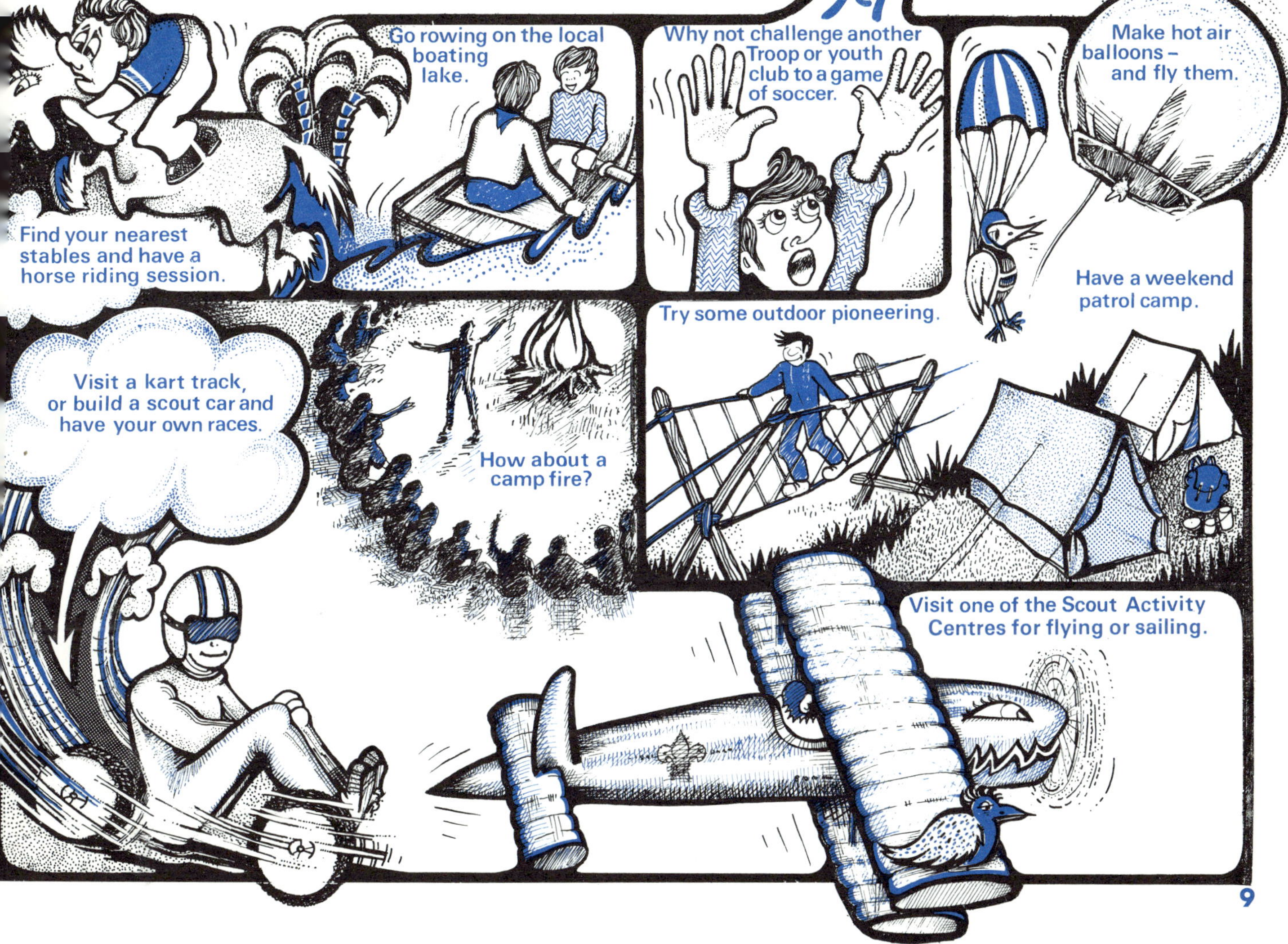
Find your nearest stables and have a horse riding session.
Go rowing on the local boating lake.
Why not challenge another Troop or youth club to a game of soccer.
Make hot air balloons – and fly them.
Have a weekend patrol camp.
Try some outdoor pioneering.
Visit a kart track, or build a scout car and have your own races.
How about a camp fire?
Visit one of the Scout Activity Centres for flying or sailing.

When you are Invested as a Scout, your Scout Leader will ask you if you know and understand the Scout Law. Then you, and all the Troop with you, will make the **Scout Sign** and you will be asked to make the Scout Promise.

Until you have made your Scout Promise you are not a Scout.

Scouts only use the Scout Sign when making or renewing their Promise. **The Scout Salute** is used at flagbreak, as a friendly greeting to another Scout or leader, when having badges presented, and when the Troop is dismissed.

Let's have a look at the Promise. You are going to promise **'On my honour . . .'** Do you know what your **honour** is? When you promise 'on your honour' it means that nothing will ever make you break your promise. You really mean it. The Knights of old would fight and even die rather than allow someone to question their honour!

You will promise 'On my honour . . . **I will do my best—'** to do **four** things. You may not always succeed, but your promise is *to do your best.* If you fail, try harder next time, don't just give up trying. If you are playing football and you don't score a goal, you try again, don't you?

THE SCOUT PROMISE

On my honour I promise that I will do my best —
To do my duty to God and to the Queen,
To help other people
And to keep the Scout Law.

THE SCOUT LAW

1
A Scout is to be trusted

2
A Scout is loyal

3
A Scout is friendly and considerate

4
A Scout is a brother to all Scouts

5
A Scout has courage in all difficulties

6
A Scout makes good use of his time and is careful of possessions and property

7
A Scout has respect for himself and for others

Let's think about the four things you will be trying your best to do:

1 To do my duty to God . . .

Really this means getting to know God, and then doing what He teaches you. It can be fun, too! You don't have to talk to Him in *special* words—you don't really need to close your eyes, especially if talking to Him whilst riding your bike! Talk to Him just like you'd do to your Dad. Of course your Dad likes to talk to you too, and you don't just talk to him when you want something, do you?

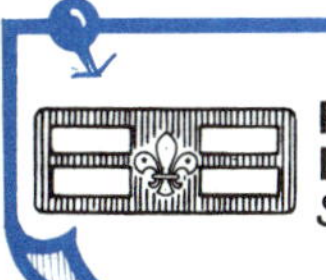

Patrol Leader—check that your Patrol Box has a modern Bible and a copy of *Scout Prayers* in it.

God can speak to you, too, in Church or Sunday School or in a **Scouts' Own** Service in camp. If you can sing, why not join the Church Choir? That can be great fun! The more you look for God, the more you'll find Him.

Why not chat with your parents and religious leader about what *your* duty to God is?

All Scouts should try to find something out about the religions of other Scouts so that they understand each other better.

If you are a Christian, let God talk to you through the Bible—get hold of a modern version that's easy to read, there's lots of them: *The Living Bible* and *Today's English Version* are just two of them, and you can get them in paperback.

2 To do my duty . . . to the Queen.

Scouts do their duty to the Queen by obeying all the laws of the land, and making sure that others do, too. We salute the **Union Flag** when it is **broken** out of respect for our Queen and country.

Making visitors to our country welcome and protecting and helping those in need are other ways you can carry out this responsibility.

3 To help other people.

If you have been a Cub Scout, you will have been trying to do a **Good Turn** to someone every day. Now that you are older you are being asked not just to do one Good Turn a day, but to be helpful all of the time.

An unknown Scout in 1909 once helped an American visitor William D. Boyce through a thick London fog. He was offered some money for the help he had given, but he refused, saying that he was a Scout and Scouts do not accept payment for being helpful. Mr Boyce was so impressed that he asked the Scout to take him to meet B.-P. at Headquarters, and as a result of this meeting Mr Boyce went back and started Scouting in the United States of America.

The boy was never traced, he just quietly disappeared when he had completed his task, and when you visit Gilwell Park you can see a **Bronze Buffalo** presented by the **Boy Scouts of America** to Britain in memory of **the unknown Scout** who kept his Promise.

The Scout Law

1 A Scout is to be trusted

Scouts are trusted to use and look after a lot of expensive and dangerous equipment such as axes, saws, pressure stoves and tents. Because you can be trusted to put it right if anything goes wrong you'll be allowed to use and do a lot of things other boys of your age wouldn't be able to do.

No Scout would dream of lying, or stealing, or cheating in games—because he can be trusted.

Your Patrol Leader, Scout Leader and parents will ask you to do a job, and then trust you to get on with it. If you don't do *your* jobs in camp, the whole Patrol might be held up in what they're doing!

2 A Scout is loyal

Do you support a football team? Then you'll be loyal to them. When you're **loyal** it means you stand by someone and help them even when things get tough. Try to be just as enthusiastic in your loyalty to your parents, school, Patrol and Troop as you are at soccer.

When you start work, perhaps a paper round, be loyal to your employer, too. If you can't make it one night, let him know so he and his customers won't be inconvenienced.

People will like you if they know you're loyal and won't let them down.

3 A Scout is friendly and considerate

When somebody new joins your Troop or Patrol, try to make them feel welcome. Ask them about their interests, invite them to tea (*ask Mum first!*) or to watch your local soccer match.

Scouts have always protected birds and animals, so be considerate when camping and don't leave things lying about that could hurt them, like broken bottles or polythene bags.

If people are rude to you, try not to be rude back. Always speak and behave politely; remember to say **'please'** and **'thank you'** and you will earn the respect of everyone you meet.

4 A Scout is a brother to all Scouts

In many countries Scouts are now wearing the purple World Badge that you will be given when you are invested. You've got brother Scouts all over the world who have made their Scout Promise just like you.

You can meet them in District or County events and competitions or at Baden-Powell House in London where Scouts from as many as 40 countries stay in a year. (See also page 7.)

If you move to another town fill in the **Transfer Form** in the back of your *Scout Progress Book* before you go and you'll find new brothers with the same interests as soon as you get there!

5 A Scout has courage in all difficulties

A recent newspaper report told of a **13-year-old** boy who kicked in two doors to rescue four children from a burning house while the adults in the street just stood and watched!

You might not be asked to show such courage, but your Scout training will help you to face danger when it comes.

Your difficulties might be schoolwork or an unkind nickname. It's easy to get discouraged, but if you can learn to say to yourself over and over again 'I can, and what's

more I *will,'* and learn to laugh **with** people even when the joke is on you, you'll suddenly find you've succeeded!

Difficulties sometimes occur at camp—perhaps your tent blowing down in the wind and rain at night. Try to make a joke of it and enjoy laughing at your troubles, and you will find things are not so bad, after all!

6 A Scout makes good use of his time and is careful of possessions and property

Did you know that the average person lives about 70 years; that's 613,000 hours! It's true!

During that period, when you add up all the separate occasions you spend an amazing amount of time doing things. You sleep for 23 years (*one third of your life*), work for 14 years, eat for 6 years, spend 8 years on leisure activities, 5 years travelling (to and from work, shops, or just around the house), talk for 4 years (*some of us more than others*) are ill for 3 years, spend 1 year on the phone (*imagine the bill!*) and 5 years dressing, bathing and shaving.

You spend 3 years doing nothing in particular and believe it or not, 80 days just looking into the mirror and 10 days blowing your nose!

During the 6 years you spend eating you'll consume 20 tons of potatoes, 18 tons of bread, 12 tons of fruit, 12 tons of vegetables, 5 tons of meat, 30,000 eggs and 1½ tons of fish!

Fantastic isn't it! So make the best use of your time—finish your homework as soon as you get home, then you will have the evening free to do other things. I wonder how much time you'll spend helping people?

Being careful of possessions and property includes that of other people as well as your own. One of the big problems in the world today concerns people defacing property with felt-tip pens, knives and paint. No Scout would ever do this: in fact a Good Turn might be to offer to clean up an area. Scouts have often cleared away rubbish and litter so that folk can enjoy their surroundings more.

7 A Scout has respect for himself and for others

This Law includes looking after your body and mind. Looking after your body is easy—most boys are soccer-mad and get lots of exercise that way in their free time as well as at school. But sometimes at camp they don't eat properly and don't go to the toilet regularly. Your body needs proper foods to keep it healthy, and while you may find camp toilets a little strange at first, *especially if they're not like the ones at home,* you'll soon get used to them. Do make sure you wash regularly, especially when preparing food—this is having respect for others who are going to eat it, too!

Respecting others includes respecting their views even if you disagree with what they say. Bullying has no place in Scouting, and is particularly important to remember if the other person is of a different race or religion.

Keeping your mind healthy includes doing your best at school and making sure that the things you think and say could be repeated in front of your parents and not embarrass anyone.

You've arrived!!

I gained my Scout Badge on

- - - - - - - - - - - - - -

Next target - - - -
Scout Standard

The Scout Standard

Many of you have joined the Scouts for the fun and challenge of going to camp. As with most skills there is a right and wrong way of camping, and Scouts have a reputation for very high camping standards. Because of this, people will allow Scouts to camp on their land when they will not allow others to do so—it is very important that you help us to keep our good name.

Scouts have a motto. It is

and the first four parts of the **Looking after yourself** section of The Scout Standard are designed to give you the training you'll need to successfully carry out the last part—camping out! So **be prepared**, and do the first four parts *before* you go camping!

Your Patrol Leader will train and test you in all of your Scout Standard requirements. We've told you that **a Scout is to be trusted,** and your Scout Leader trusts your Patrol Leader to keep a high standard and to make sure you do the tests properly.

At the same time, if you have the opportunity to pass an **Advanced Scout Standard** test while you are working through the Scout Standard you don't have to wait until you've finished the Scout Standard. Take the opportunity—

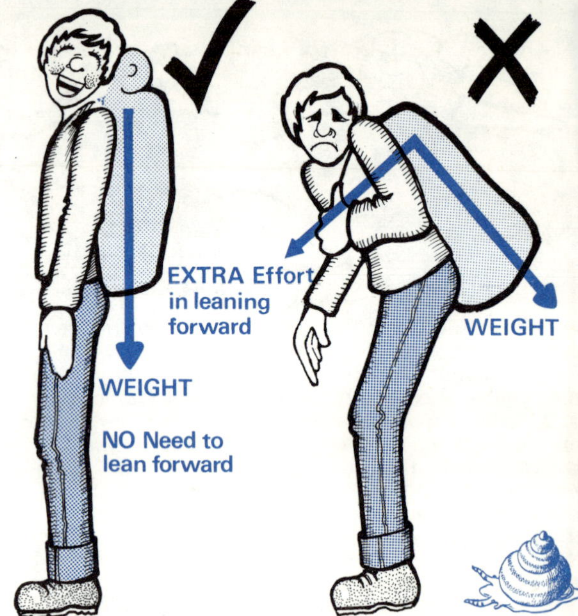

your Scout Leader makes the arrangements for Advanced Scout Standard tests (he can invite an experienced Patrol Leader to test you if he wishes), so discuss it with Skip, and we'll try to show you suitable opportunities as you read this book.

If you haven't yet got a rucsac these next few paragraphs are designed to suggest the best buys. **Don't** buy *any* rucsac just because it's cheap—make sure you get the right kind.

The old-fashioned type (above right) tends to pull you over backwards and is much more tiring than the modern rucsac (above left) which keeps the load high up so that the weight acts vertically over the spine. This arrangement, if properly worn, is better in every way. Whether you buy a rucsac with a frame or not depends on your pocket and preference, but most people prefer the frame-type.

Patrol Leader—try to arrange a visit to your local Scout Shop or camping store to show your Patrol the kinds of rucsac available. Your Patrol Box should have a copy of Scout Shops Ltd.'s camping catalogue which illustrates many different types of rucsac.

Patrol Activity—try to obtain as many different types of rucsac as possible, load them with normal camping equipment and try a six-mile hike, each person changing rucsacs every mile so that you can compile a *Which?* report on rucsacs.

How NOT to pack a rucsac

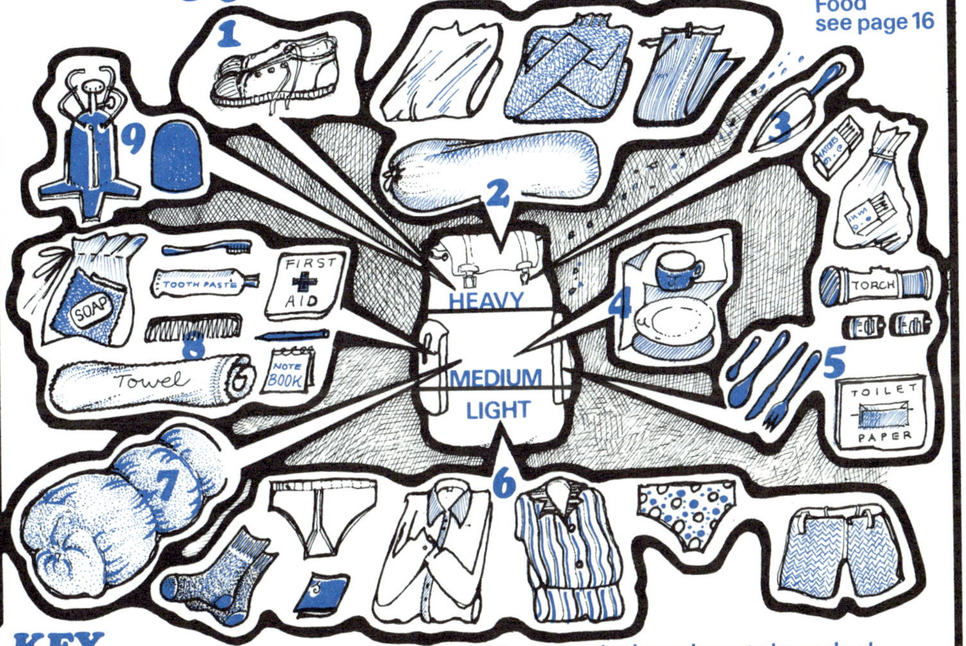

1 Plimsolls or Training shoes.
2 Waterproof cape, warm sweater. jeans and tent.
3 Trowel (for digging toilet).
4 Unbreakable plates and mug.
5 Cutlery, torch, spare batteries, matches and toilet paper.
6 Spare clothes, underclothes, handkerchiefs, socks, swim-wear and pyjamas.
7 Sleeping bag.
8 Towel, soap, toothbrush, tooth-paste, flannel, first aid kit notebook – pencil.
9 Stove and extra fuel.

Packing your Rucsac

▶ Put in FIRST what you want LAST !!!

Food see page 16

HEAVY

MEDIUM

LIGHT

KEY . . .

Pack in polythene bags to keep dry !

When you pack your rucsac put everything inside it, not hanging from it like a Christmas tree! Things are easier to pack and find if folded properly. Make sure fuel, *especially paraffin* is sealed and cannot leak or taint food.

Some folk pack everything in like books on a shelf, but most people pack everything flat. Put soft material at the back of your sac so that sharp edges won't dig into you.

See the *Advanced Scout Standard* book for help with weight limits. After camp, note what you didn't use, then next time don't take it—apart from washing and first aid kits!

A Scout is **careful of possessions and property**, so when you've learned how to pack a rucsac, learn how to pack your drawers at home and how to pack a suitcase for family holidays. **Mark everything with your name.**

Idea for Patrol Leader:

Demonstration 'Do it yourself' Rucsac.

Make a rucsac out of polythene and use it to demonstrate how it should be packed without having to open it.

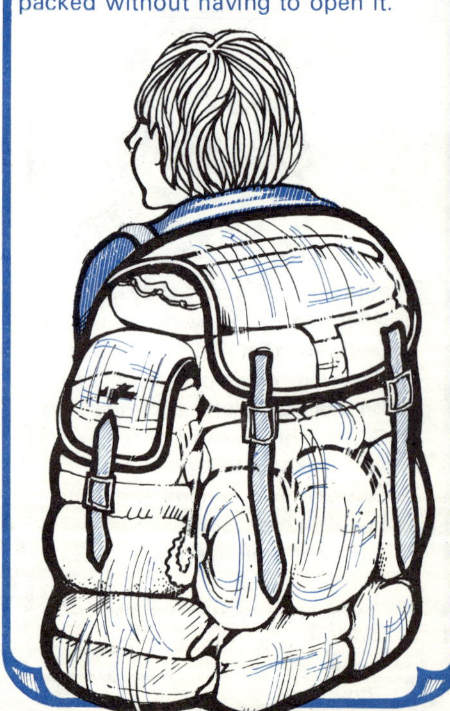

Looking after yourself

(b) Prepare a personal first aid kit for an expedition.

Prepared sterile dressings for minor burns, etc.

—two finger size,
—one medium
—one large

Prepared plasters (adhesive dressings)

—12 assorted shapes and sizes. Keep in small tin. *Some people are allergic to plasters.*

Antiseptic solution

—eg. Dettol, T.C.P.
—add to water when washing dirty wounds
—keep in polythene bottle.

Triangular Bandage

—use to protect contents of kit
—main use in supporting broken limbs
See *Advanced Scout Standard* book.

Sterilised cotton wool

—½ oz. pack
—for cleaning wounds.

THIS KIT IS MEANT TO BE USED Keep it stocked up and always take it on hikes!

Table salt

—one teaspoonful sealed in small plastic bag
—use for sterilizing solution or to counteract heat exhaustion. *Find out how.*

Safety pins

—3, medium size

Tweezers (Forceps)

—useful for removing splinters.

Darning needle

—sterilize before use
—use for removing splinters.

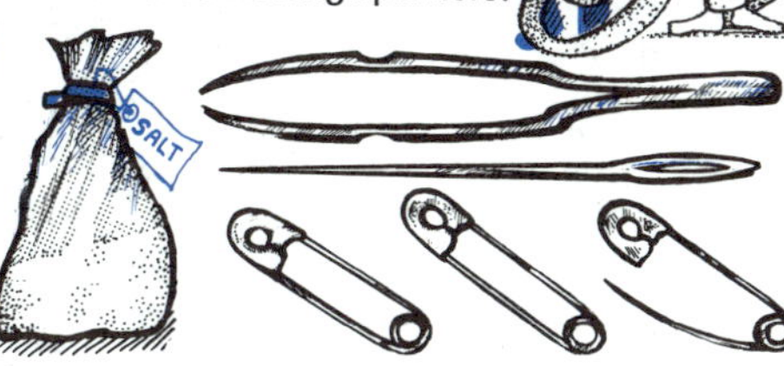

Scissors

—one sided razorblade may be used as alternative. *Keep in original pack.*
—keep scissors dry to prevent rusting. *Use polythene bag.*

Card

—with your name, address, and telephone number on it, and details of any special medical condition, eg. diabetes or haemophilia.

Coins

—one 2p coin and one 10p coin in case of urgent telephone call
—**remember 999 calls are free and that you can 'reverse charges' through the operator if you have no money and the person you want to contact will accept the charge.**

Book Matches

—sealed in plastic bag for lighting a fire in an emergency to provide warmth or making hot drinks.

The *Advanced Scout Standard* book and pages 27 to 29 will show you how to use these items properly.

Looking after Yourself

(c) Light a fire; make a hot drink; cook a simple meal out-of-doors.

Kindling should be absolutely dry, dead leaves dead grass, dried orange peel, paper, birch bark etc.

Next, the thinnest of dead twigs, drier if snapped off the tree than picked off the ground, then thicker and thicker twigs.

Preparing the ground

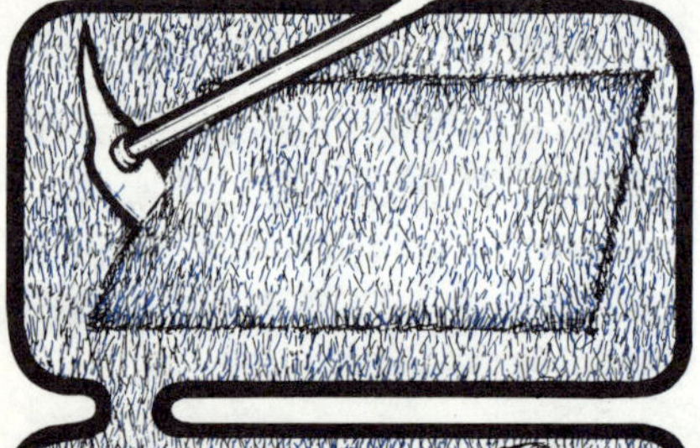

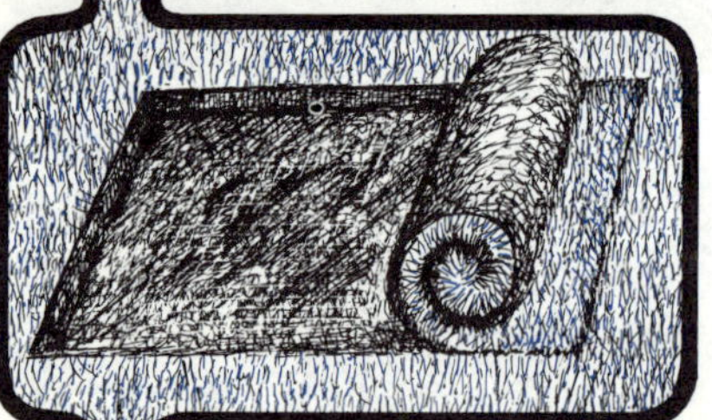

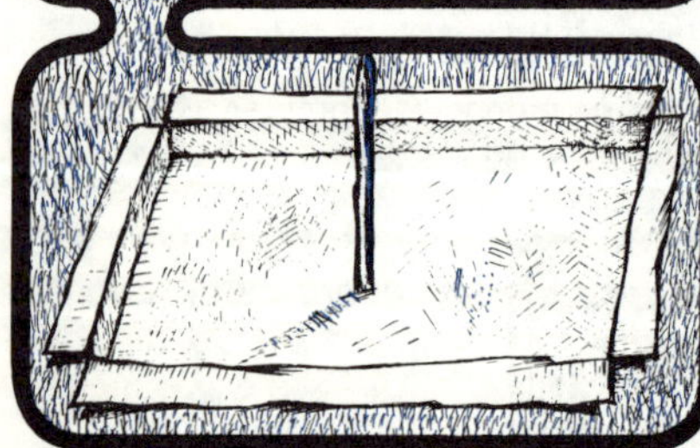

When choosing your fireplace select an area at least 3 metres (10 ft.) from the nearest hedge or bush, with no over-hanging branches from trees. This is to prevent sparks spreading the fire.

Cut an area of turf approximately one metre by a half-metre, using an entrenching tool. **Rolling** the turf is an easy way of removing it. Try to keep the turf in one piece and store it flat, roots uppermost, in a cool damp place.

The amount you remove should be sufficient to prevent the surrounding grass from charring.

In a long camp you should water the grass regularly to keep it in good condition.

If the ground is damp you can line the fireplace with cooking foil to give a dry foundation for your fire.

A small stake pushed into the ground to build the fire round will help support the materials.

You can always find dry wood however wet the weather by looking for dead twigs or branches (leafless) on trees. They should snap off *immediately* they are bent. If they don't they are not dead.

Always *build* your fire—don't just heap it up. **Read the section of this book on use of axe and knife.** (Pages 41–42).

Shield the fire from the wind until it has caught well, after which the wind will help it to burn.

Have fuel on hand to replenish the fire before you light it.

Never stick an axe into a tree or chop branches off trees without permission.

Different Ways of Supporting Cooking Utensils ...

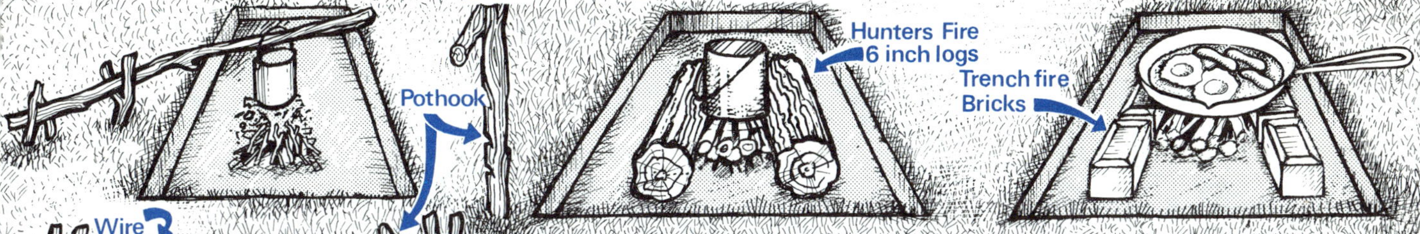

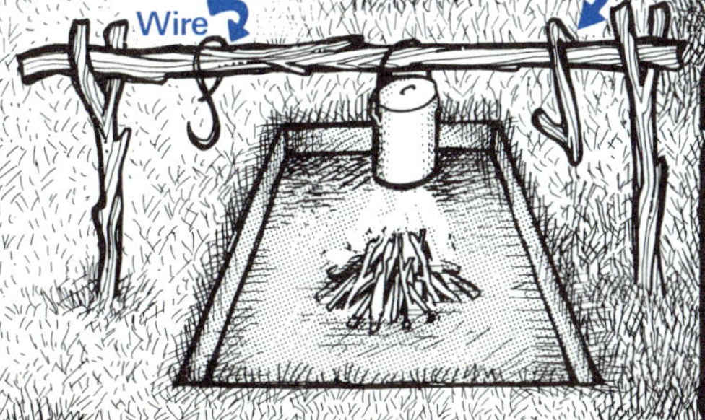

Wire

Pothook

Hunters Fire
6 inch logs

Trench fire
Bricks

Burning Values of Wood K=KINDLING C=COOKING Good★★★ Average★★ Bad★

Wood	K	C
Ash	K – ★★	C – ★★★
Beech	K – ★★	C – ★★
Birch	K – ★★★	C – ★★★
Horse Chestnut	K – ★	C – ★
Sweet Chestnut	K – ★	C – ★★
Elm	K – ★	C – ★
Hawthorn	K – ★★★	C – ★★★
Hazel	K – ★★	C – ★★
Holly	K – ★★★	C – ★★★
Larch	K – ★★★	C – ★★★
Lime	K – ★★	C – ★★
Oak	K – ★	C – ★★
Pine	K – ★★★	C – ★★★
Poplar	K – ★	C – ★
Spruce	K – ★★★	C – ★★★
Sycamore	K – ★	C – ★★

Meals You Can Cook ...

Sausages on a peeled stick cooked over glowing embers or in a frying pan with a little fat.

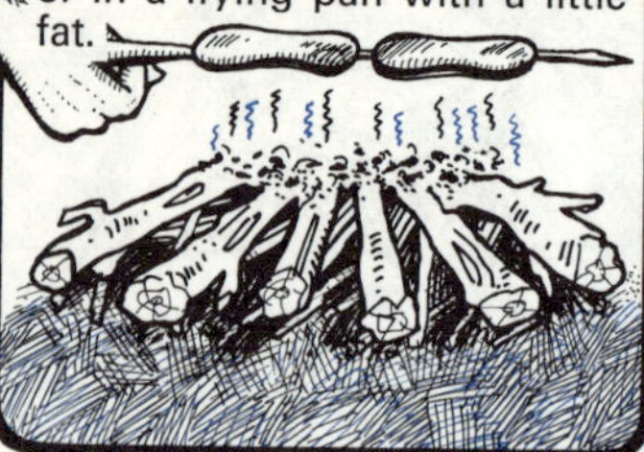

Fish in foil with a little butter, cooked in embers.

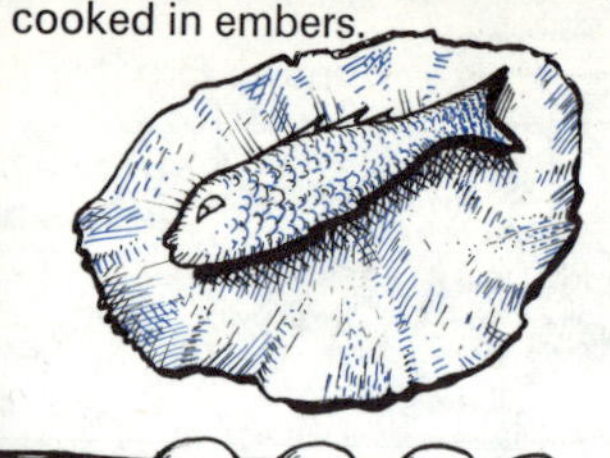

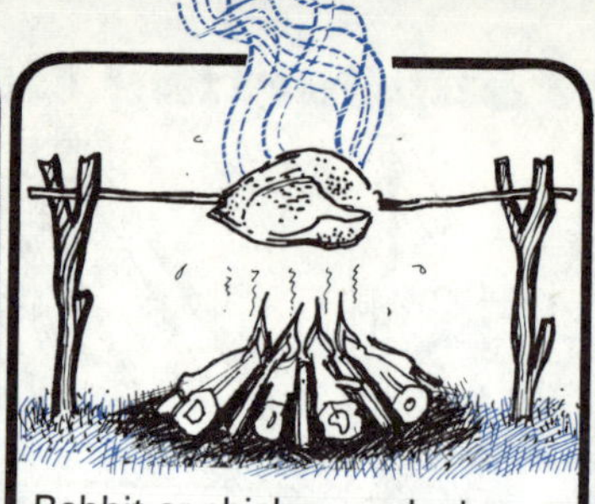

Rabbit or chicken cooked on a spit.

Page 26 of *Enjoy Camping* published by The Scout Association, will give you more ideas for meals. See also the *Advanced Scout Standard* book and *Chief Scout's Award* book.

A Scout has respect for himself and for others comes into cooking in making sure food is fresh and cooked and served properly.

This Scout Law, and **being careful of possessions and property,** are two important things to remember whenever you light or clear up a fire.

You'll learn other ways of cooking including how to use a pressure stove when you do your Advanced Scout Standard.

Practice cooking at home—it's no fun starving at camp because you haven't learned to cook!

Egg and bacon or chops.

Potatoes baked in foil in embers.

Twists

Make a stiff dough of flour and water and a pinch of salt. Peel the end of a thick green stick and heat it on the fire to dry the sap and help with the cooking. Make your dough into a long narrow snake, wrap it round the *hot* stick and bake it over the embers. You should be able to slide the twist off when it is cooked. Serve with jam.

Pigeon or chicken in clay or foil and cooked in embers.

Boiled eggs or potatoes.

When your fire is finished remove the ash and foil, loosen the soil with a stick, water it and replace the turf.

When you leave there should be no sign of where you have been!

Drinks

Tea

Oxo

Coffee

Horlicks

Soup

Cocoa

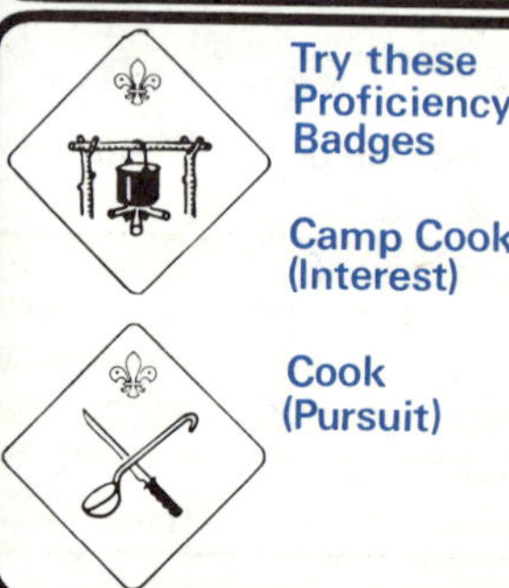

Try these Proficiency Badges

Camp Cook (Interest)

Cook (Pursuit)

Looking after Yourself
(d) Pitch and strike a hike tent.

Patrol Leader—do remember that this test is for hike tents, not Patrol tents. As there are so many different types of hike tent, try to borrow a selection other than your usual ones (from another Troop, perhaps) and invite your Patrol to erect them and say which they like best.

Types of Hike Tent

Basic Hike Tent
Approximate weight 2½-3½ kg. (5-7½ lb.)
Cost £30 to £60.
Available with or without sewn-in groundsheet and with or without flysheet.

A-Pole Hike Tent
Approximate weight 4½ kg. (9 lb.)
Cost £35 to £50.
Only suitable for advanced campers.

'Good Companions' Type
Approximate weight 3-5 kg. (6½-10 lb.)
Cost £65 to £90.
Available with or without sewn-in groundsheet, with or without flysheet, and with A-poles or other supports.

Pitching the Tent

1

2

Whether your tent has a sewn-in groundsheet or not, start by pegging out the groundsheet.

If the tent has a separate groundsheet, you will now have to peg the corners of the tent down to fit the groundsheet.

Assemble the upright poles, and the ridge-pole if your tent has one. The ridge-pole usually goes inside the tent, so slide it into place now.

Put the spike of the front upright through the ridge-pole hole and the corresponding hole in the tent.

See Scout Shops Ltd's Catalogue for a variety of different types of tent.

There are now basically two methods in common use. Either: stand the front pole upright, enter the tent and put the rear upright pole through the ridge and tent-hole and stand that upright.

Or: keep the front pole lying on the ground through the ridge and tent holes, wriggle into the tent and insert the rear upright pole through the ridge and tent-hole, come out of the tent and with a partner, raise both poles together. **This method is often preferred because it prevents the ridge pole and spike being twisted.**

You will soon find in Scouting that everyone has their own favourite method of tent pitching and you can find details of different ways of pitching different tents on pages 7-9 of *Enjoy Camping.*

Experienced campers always knock in the pegs for the corner guys early on—*you can always move them if you find they are not quite right*—so that they can loop the corner guy lines over the pegs and stand the tent up on its own whilst they finish off the job of pegging out the guy lines.

Side lines should always be in line with the seams and the guy should come away from the peg at right-angles. You will save yourself a lot of trouble if **before** you peg out the corner guys you fasten the doors of the tent so that they will be sure to meet when you have finished erecting the tent.

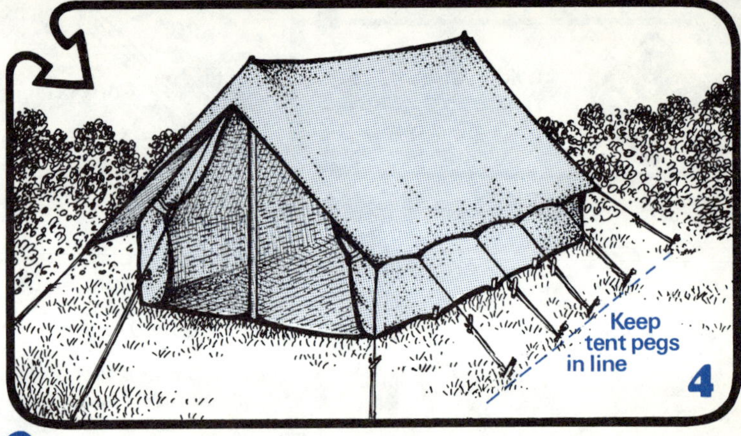

Having pegged out the guys, the main guylines should be hooked over the spikes (if they are not permanently attached to the tent) and drawn taught.

Flysheets are attached in many different ways. With some tents the main ridge is put outside instead of inside and the tent supported by loops sewn on top. On other tents there are **ridge-separators** to fit over the main pole spikes and an additional ridge-pole to fit across them.

Whichever method is used, the flysheet fits over the horizontal pole and is pegged down. **It should not come into contact with the tent underneath.**

Flysheets don't keep out flies! They keep out heavy rain and by trapping a layer of air between the sheet and tent, help to keep the tent cool in summer and warm in winter.

If your tent doesn't have a flysheet you *must* make sure that you **don't rub against the roof in rain** or it will come through and wet the contents of the tent—and that might be you!

Care

A damp tent will rot and become mildewed, so dry it *at once*—don't leave it a week, or that will be too late.

You are responsible for the care of tents loaned to you. Repair any tears or broken guy-lines, your Patrol Leader or Quartermaster will show you how, before somebody has their camp spoiled by finding out the hard way that *you've* forgotten! (**A Scout is a brother to all Scouts**).

Striking

When striking camp (packing everything away) always drop your tent **into** the wind, otherwise you might end up flying a rather large kite!

If your tent has a sewn-in groundsheet leave it pegged down until the tent is ready for folding. If the groundsheet is separate it sometimes helps in a high wind if you leave the **leeward** guys fastened down until the tent is laid on the ground. This will stop the tent from lifting up.

The removal of metal tent pegs, used with most hike tents, is similar to that of the wooden pegs as shown.

Lever backwards and forwards to slacken off, then pull up.

Make a 'patent' tent-peg extractor.

Pivot

methods of removing tent pegs

Folding and Packing

Different tents are folded in different ways: your Patrol Leader will show you how to pack yours. Don't forget to **clean the pegs** which should be packed in a separate bag and never placed in contact with the tent canvas. *Always count the pegs* so that the next user will have enough. Tell the Quartermaster if any are lost so he can replace them.

If it is raining when you pack your tent, you *must* make sure that you unpack it when you arrive back and hang it up to dry.

Looking after Yourself

(e) Camp out for at least one night or, in winter, spend at least one night in a hostel or hut as part of a Scout activity.

In this book we are going to deal with a simple two-man camp. The *Advanced Scout Standard* book deals with **standing** camps and the *Chief Scout's Award* book deals with **hike** camping.

It is probable that most Scouts will pass this test whilst camping with their Patrol, but some of the more adventurous types will want to camp with just one or two other Scouts. You've been learning to **look after yourself** and now is your chance to prove you can do just that!

Simple Two-man Camp Site

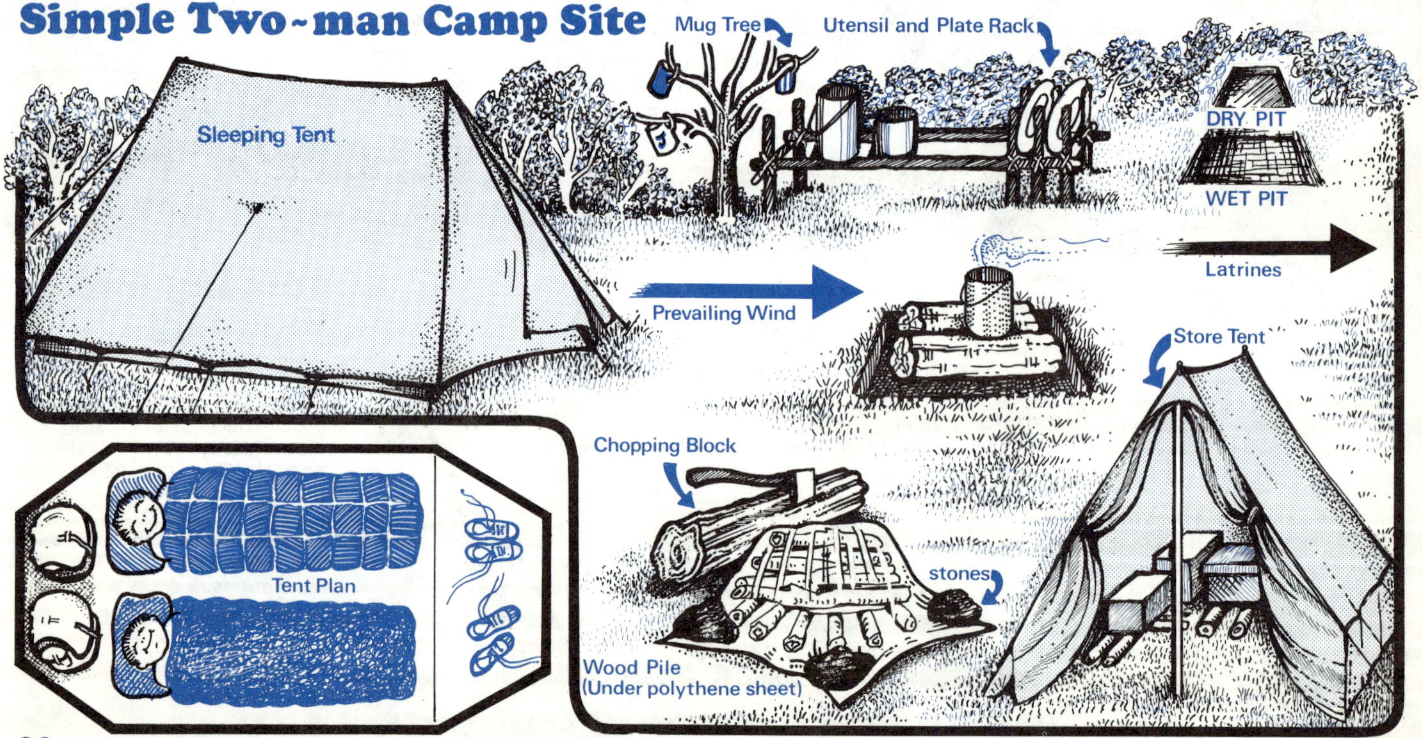

These proficiency badges are all linked with camping — look them up!

Camp cook (Interest)	**Camper** (Pursuit)	**Explorer** (Pursuit)

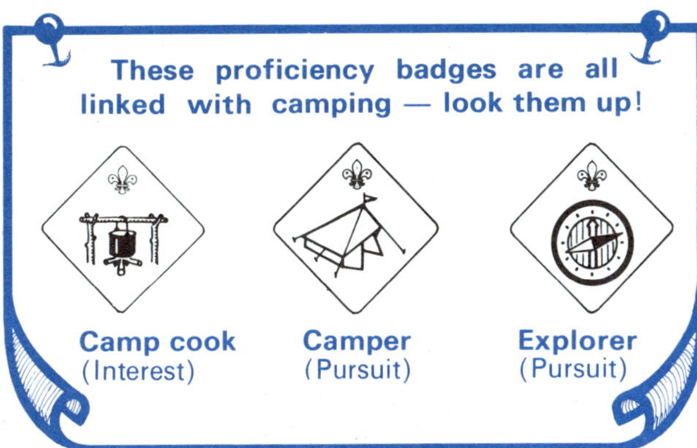

If you've never been away from home before, camp might be a real test of your keeping of the 5th. Scout Law: **A Scout has courage in all difficulties**—especially if the weather turns bad, or you are woken one night by a friendly cow trying to enter your tent!

It would be a good idea to pass the **Handaxe and Knife** section of The Scout Standard *before* this camp so that you'll know how to use them properly.

A few tips . . .

. . . unless your guylines are self-adjusting or nylon, slacken them off at night because if it rains they will shrink and may break—and your tent will collapse.

. . . keep all food in sealed containers and off the ground unless you want all the squirrels, hedgehogs, beetles and other 'inhabitants' of your site to have supper while you sleep!

. . . always put your fire out at night—if the wind gets up and sparks fly, your tent may catch fire with fatal results for you!

. . . many camp sites no longer allow you to dig wet and dry pits—check with the camp warden, the farmer or the land owner.

. . . read *Enjoy Camping.* It is easy to understand and tells you everything you need to know about camping in the Scouts.

Things to do at Camp

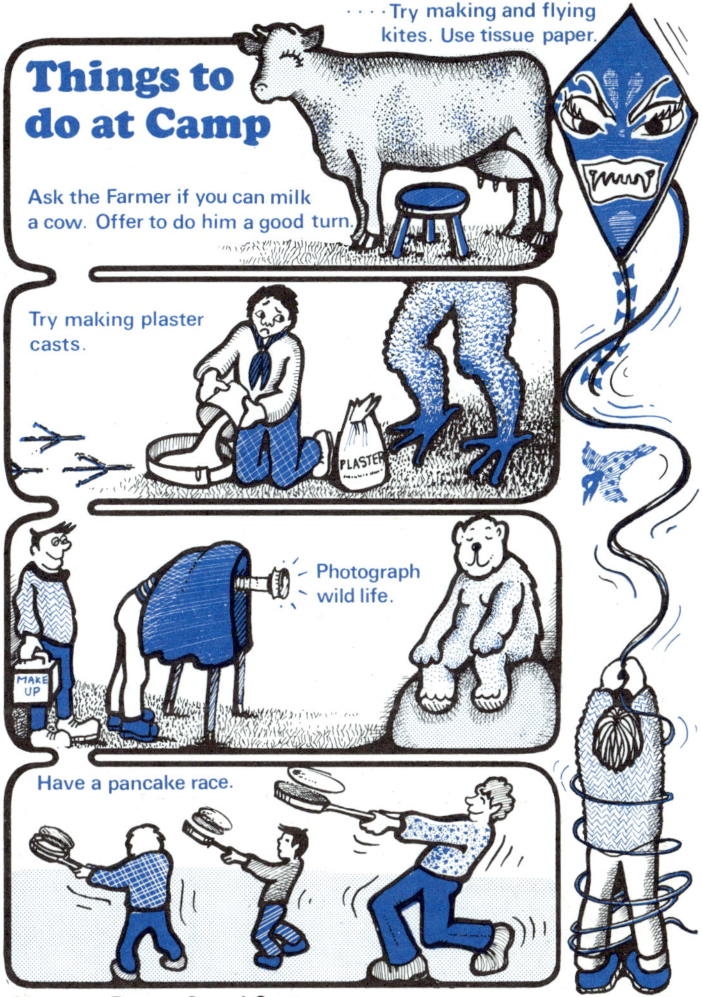
. . . . Try making and flying kites. Use tissue paper.
Ask the Farmer if you can milk a cow. Offer to do him a good turn.
Try making plaster casts.
PLASTER
MAKE UP
Photograph wild life.
Have a pancake race.

Also see Pages 8 and 9 ←

So who needs a Tent?

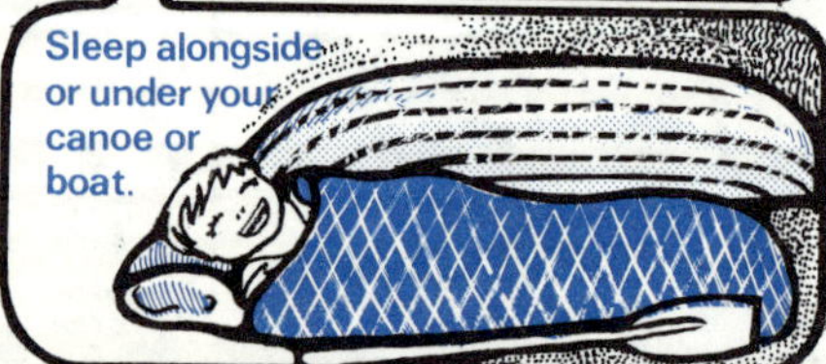

If you go hiking, or travel by other means, you'll want to travel light. You'll be doing an expedition in your **Advanced Scout Standard,** but you may like to sleep out before then.

Most Scout camp sites have huts or other accommodation that is available for use in winter or bad weather, ranging from simple wooden huts to veritable palaces!

Don't just camp in summer—try some winter camping, either in a Scout hut, or, if you're a tough guy—*under canvas*!

There are over 400 Youth Hostels all over the British Isles and some 3,000 throughout Europe!

All of them provide overnight accommodation for hikers at very cheap rates. You can either buy your meals or cook your own. Youth Hostels range from old castles to converted farm buildings in all the popular and not-so-popular areas. Full details from: **The Youth Hostels Association, Trevelyan House, St. Albans, Hertfordshire.**

Baden-Powell House was opened by Her Majesty The Queen in July 1961 and is open to all members of the Scout Movement. Cubs, Scouts and Leaders saved for years to bring this magnificent centre into being. It has single, twin and family rooms, dormitories, restaurant, T.V. room, showers and many other amenities. Write to **The Warden, Baden-Powell House, Queen's Gate, London SW7 5JS,** for full details. Have a Patrol or Troop weekend in London and meet Scouts from all over the world!

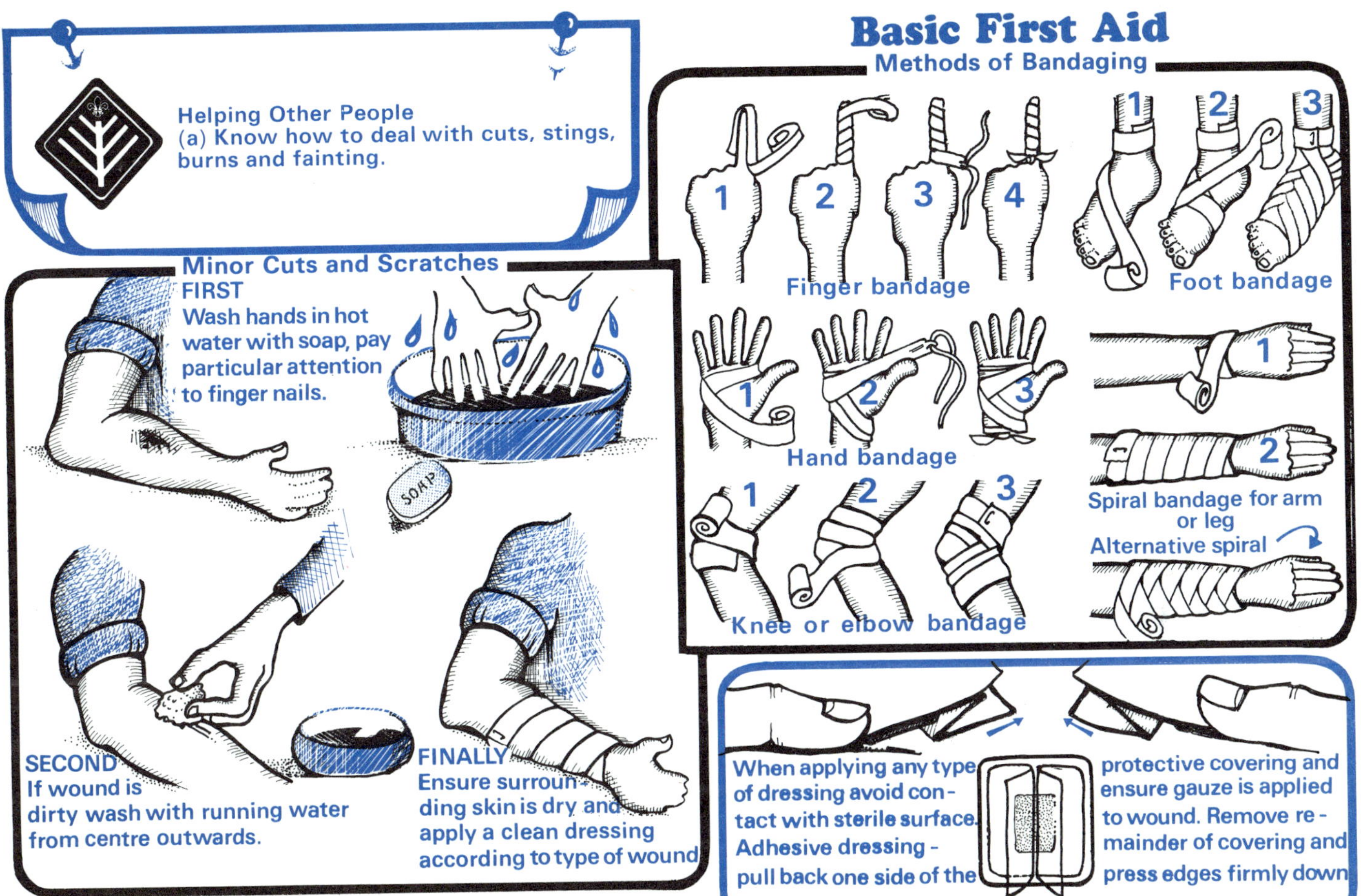

This section shows how to use the FIRST AID KIT shown on page 17

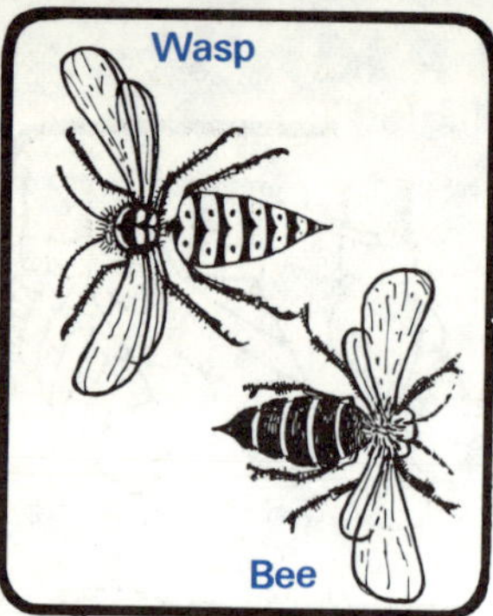

Stings

Bees, hornets and wasps.

(1) Remove the sting, if present, using tweezers or the point of a needle that has been sterilized by passing it through a flame **and then cooling it.** (*This only usually applies to Bee stings*).

(2) Antihistamine creams or sprays are useful if applied *immediately*. Otherwise, apply surgical spirit or a **weak** solution of ammonia, or a solution of bicarbonate of soda.

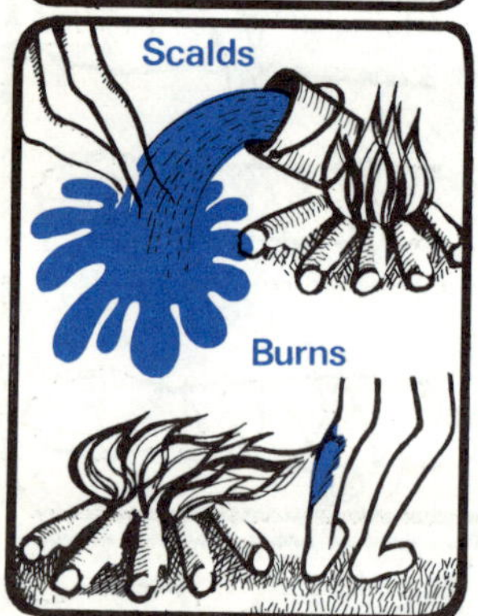

(3) If the sting is in the mouth give a mouthwash of one teaspoonful of bicarbonate of soda to a tumbler of water. If there is much swelling in the mouth or difficulty in breathing place the casualty in the **recovery position** (see *Advanced Scout Standard* book) and give ice to suck.

Stings in the mouth, ear or any sensitive area should always be taken to the doctor. Look for signs of shock.

Burns and Scalds

Burns may be caused by dry heat, fire, hot objects, exposure to sun, chemicals (eg. in the school lab.) electricity (see *Advanced Scout Standard* book), or friction (eg. by sliding down a rope too fast). Scalds are caused by wet heat, eg. steam or boiling water. **Treatment is the same for both.**

Aims: (1) to reduce the effect of the heat; (2) to relieve pain; (3) to prevent infection; (4) to ensure proper medical treatment is given later.

What to do:

(1) Place the burn or scald under slowly running cold water or immerse the part in cool water, keeping it there for 10 minutes, or until the pain ceases.

(2) Remove at once any tightly fitting articles—bangles, belts, boots, rings etc. before swelling occurs.

(3) **Carefully** remove clothing soaked in boiling water, but do not remove burned clothing.

(4) Lay or sit the casualty down depending on how severe and where the burn/scald is.

(5) Make sure your hands are clean and avoid contact with the injured areas as much as possible.

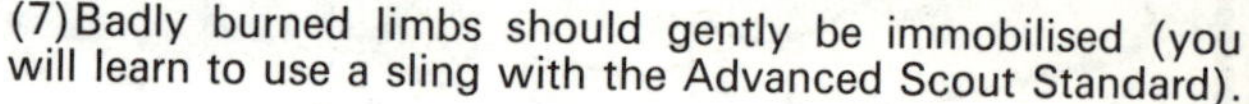

(6) Cover the injured area with a **sterile** dressing (a clean sheet, or freshly laundered item will do as an alternative—**the object is to exclude air and therefore infection**). With facial burns a breathing hole may be necessary in the dressing.

(7) Badly burned limbs should gently be immobilised (you will learn to use a sling with the Advanced Scout Standard).

(8) Give **small cold drinks** at frequent intervals to a badly burned casualty **only if they are conscious**.

(9) Arrange for a badly burned or scalded casualty to go straight to hospital.

(10) Talk cheerfully to the casualty reassuring him all the time. Avoid leaving him alone.

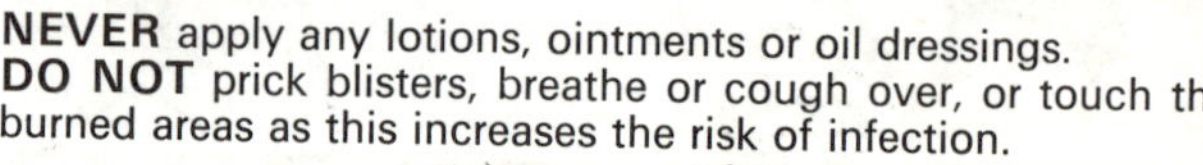

NEVER apply any lotions, ointments or oil dressings.
DO NOT prick blisters, breathe or cough over, or touch the burned areas as this increases the risk of infection.

Sunburn

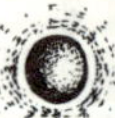

Place the casualty in the shade, and give a cold drink. Various lotions such as calamine lotion are available for slight irritations or redness, but if the sunburn is severe seek medical aid.

To avoid sunburn you should expose your skin to the sun for short (5–10 min.) periods gradually increasing as you become adapted.

Always protect your head and the back of your neck. Oily sun-tan lotions, sunbathing wet with sea-water or sweat, aggravate burns.

Fainting

Fainting is caused by a temporary blood shortage in the brain, usually the result of some form of emotional or physical shock or exhaustion.

Treatment of a faint

(1) Lay the casualty down and raise the legs slightly above the level of the head.
(2) See that he has plenty of fresh air and put him in the shade if necessary.
(3) Loosen clothing at neck, chest and waist.
(4) If breathing is difficult place him in the recovery position (see *Advanced Scout Standard* book).
(5) Reassure him as he regains consciousness.
(6) Gradually raise him into the sitting position and give sips of water if requested.

NOTE: If the patient does not recover fairly soon, obtain medical aid—it may not be a simple faint.

Avoiding a faint

If a person is about to faint they will usually complain of feeling ill or giddy. The face usually becomes pale or greenish-white in colour and beads of sweat will be seen on face, neck and hands.
(1) Reassure him and urge him to breathe deeply, and to flex the muscles of the legs, thighs and buttocks to help blood circulation.
(2) Loosen clothing at neck, chest and waist.
(3) Lay him down in a current of fresh air or make him sit with his head between his knees.
(4) On recovery, sips of water may be given.
(5) If smelling salts are used test the strength yourself before use.

Check and treat the casualty for any injuries he may have sustained in falling.

Dog bites and cuts from rusty wire or nails should always be checked by a doctor because of risk of infection.

Patrol Leader—First Aid is *not* a game, and the highest standards should be insisted upon. A Scout may need to know First Aid at camp, at home, in school or anywhere, and if he is alone a life may depend on how well you trained him! (Re-read page 12—5th. Scout Law notes).

Summoning help

Remember you are not a doctor! Send for expert help (or take the casualty there) as soon as possible. Say:

Where the accident is.
What has happened.
What you have done.
Who you are.
Who (if anyone) sent you.

Ambulance (Service)

Aim to get this badge as soon as possible.

Helping other people

(b) Show ability to direct strangers and have some knowledge of local public transport services and local places of interest or importance, including the location of doctors, police station, fire alarms and public call-boxes.

When you made your Scout Promise you promised to **help other people**, and this part of the **Scout Standard** teaches you how to do this. You've learnt some First Aid, but people don't just require help when they are injured!

People will stop you and ask directions. Sometimes you will know the answer, sometimes you won't.

Giving directions may seem easy, but can be difficult. If the person is driving a car *don't* send them down back streets and through fields! Direct them along main roads, even if it is not the quickest way. Mention landmarks, or the distance to turnings.

'Turn left along Kingsway' means the driver will keep taking his eyes off the road to look at street signs, but if you say 'Kingsway's opposite a school' or 'half-a-mile down the road' he'll drive more safely.

When the route is complicated give directions for part of the journey and suggest they should then 'ask again'.

Never go with a stranger in his car—nearly every week young people are attacked by strangers who ask them to go in their cars.

Scouts *must not* 'hitch' lifts on hikes partly for this reason. People say 'It'll never happen to me'—**but for some it has**.

Patrol Leader—how about arranging a treasure hunt or cycle (horse?) ride around town to visit all the important places. Some people rarely get beyond their own street!

Guide (Service)

This proficiency badge is linked with this part of The Scout Standard. Why not try for it?

Historical Buildings

Churches

Library

Museums

Zoo

Post Box

Make Your Own List Now!

Local doctor ____________________

____

____

Local dentist ____________________

____

____

Local clinic ____________________

____

____

Local hospital ____________________

____

____

Local post-office and post-boxes ____________________

____

____

Local railway stations (inc. Underground if there is one in your area)

____

____

Local coach/bus stations

____

____

Local Churches ____________________

____

C. of E. ____________________

____

R.C. ____________________

____

Baptist ____________________

____

Methodist ____________________

____

Others ____________________

____

Local Police Station ____________________

____

Local Fire Alarm/Fire Brigade ____________________

____

Local Rescue Services (eg. Lifeboat, Mountain Rescue, etc.) ____________________

____

Local restaurants/cafes

____

Local public houses ____________________

____

____

Petrol stations: ____________________

All night ____________________

Others ____________________

____

Car repair garages ____________________

____

____

Local shopping centre ____________________

____

____

Public car parks ____________________

____

Public telephone boxes

____

Places of Interest ____________________

____

Town Hall ____________________

____

Public library ____________________

____

Zoo ____________________

____

Museum ____________________

____

Park ____________________

____

Swimming pool ____________________

____

Others ____________________

____

____

____

Getting About

(a) **Set a map; know what is meant by a compass bearing.**
(b) **Show understanding of scale and conventional signs by describing a short route selected on an Ordnance Survey map.**

You may not know it, but you can buy **dozens** of different types of maps of the same area, from road maps to the stars visible at different times!

The purpose for which you intend to use the map decides which you will buy.

Scouts usually use **Ordnance Survey** maps because of their accuracy and detail. The most popular are:

1:50 000 (2cm = 1km)
1:25 000 (4cm = 1km)

Two extracts showing the same area appear opposite so you can compare the detail shown.

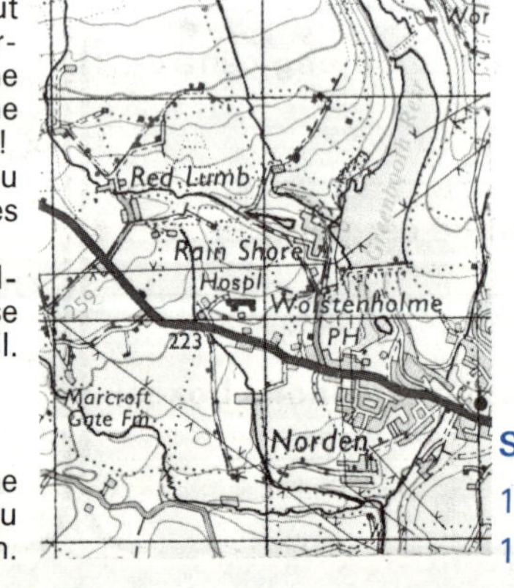

Scale

1:50 000 ←
1:25 000 →

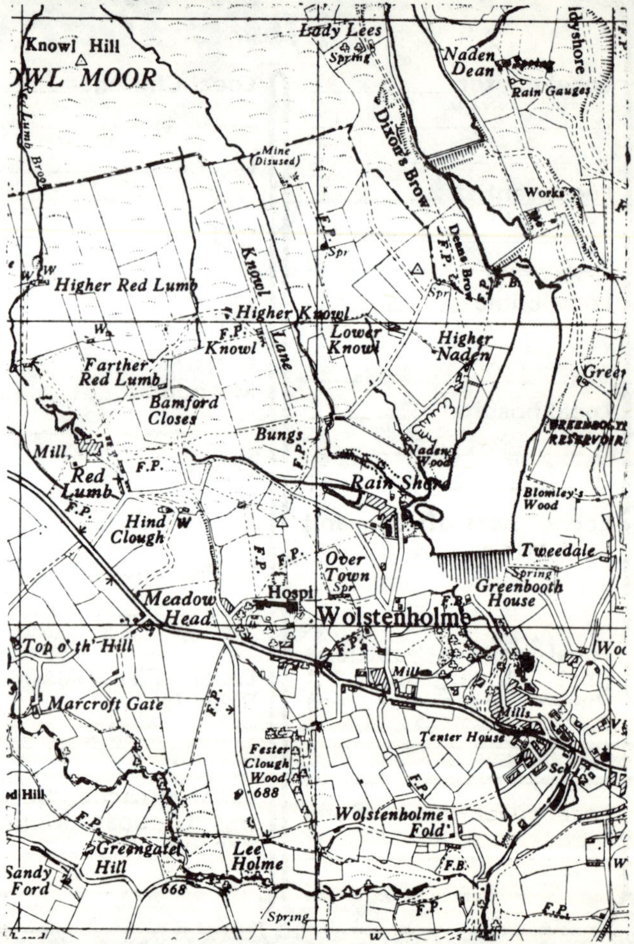

Patrol Leader—did you know that any Troop can have Sea Scouts and Air Scouts in it? You can have Patrols of each, or follow the Sea and/or Air Training Programmes as ordinary Scouts.

Sea Scouts and **Air Scouts** will eventually learn about how to read and use oceanic and waterway maps or air traffic route maps as well as O.S. maps.

(See the **Coxswain Badge** and **Senior** or **Master Airman Badges,** which you may attempt when you have started work on the **Advanced Scout Standard).**

The first thing to learn about reading a map is having it the 'right way round', and to do this you need to learn to find North, so we'll do this first!

Finding North

1 Using the SUN

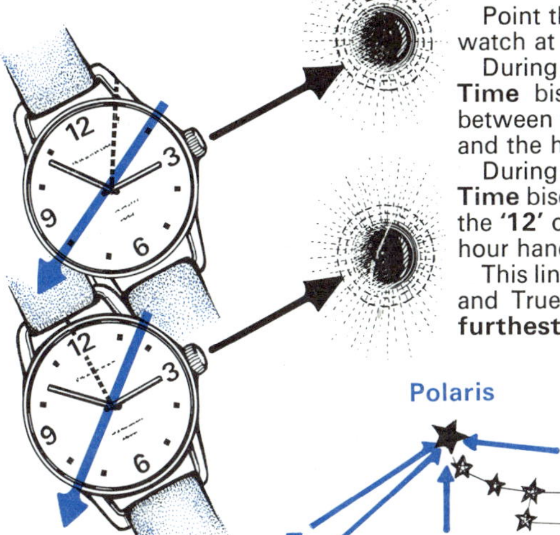

Point the **hour** hand of your watch at the sun.

During **British Summer Time** bisect (half) the angle between the **'1'** on your watch and the hour hand.

During **Greenwich Mean Time** bisect the angle between the **'12'** on your watch and the hour hand.

This line points North-South, and True North is at the end **furthest** from the sun.

Polaris

Ursa Minor
(Little Bear)

The Plough
(part of Ursa Major)

Cassiopeia

Orion

2 Using the STARS

To find True North at night you must find **Polaris** (the Pole Star) which is situated over the Earth's North Pole. The easiest way is to use one of the constellations illustrated above as shown. Once you have found it you will have to estimate other directions. To hike North, just keep heading for Polaris.

3 Using the COMPASS

There are 3 kinds of North

The Silva Compass

The two methods we have discussed so far give you **True North**.

Your compass needle points to **Magnetic North**, which is quite different, and Ordnance Survey Maps have their own North called **Grid North**. (Your Patrol Leader will explain this.)

On every Ordnance Survey map there is an **Orientation** panel which explains the relative positions of these and how to allow for the fact that the Magnetic North Pole moves around. The Orientation panel from the 1:50 000 O.S. map on page 38 appears below.

Orientation

NORTH POINTS Difference of true north from grid north at sheet corners

N W corner	N E corner	S W corner	S E corner
1° 29′ W	1° 56′ W	1° 27′ W	1° 54′ W

Magnetic north about 8·5° W of grid north in 1974 decreasing by about 0·5° in eight years

Grid North
True North
Magnetic North
Diagrammatic only

300° 040° 135°

Bearings

Bearings are usually measured from **Grid North,** and consist of the angle measured clockwise from Grid North to where you want to go.

Bearings always consist of **3** figures, so angles of less than 100° have zeros placed in front, e.g. 040°.

Setting your Map

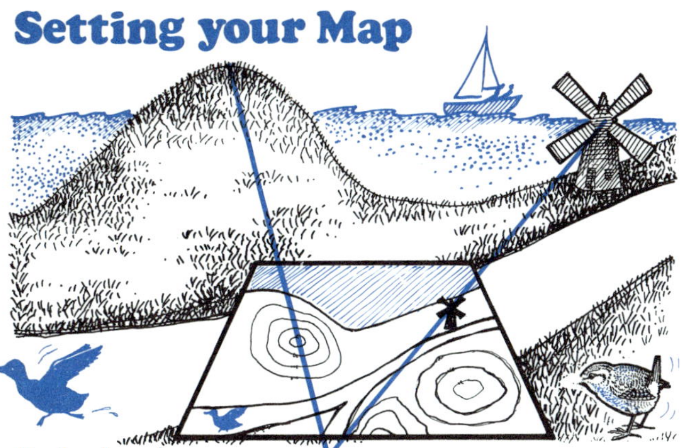

By landmarks

Choose two landmarks that are a fair distance apart and line them up with their symbols on the map. (See any 1:50 000 O.S. map for explanation of symbols). This method is quite simple, but beware of similar-looking features. A third landmark is a good check once you think you've got it right!

By stars

Use the method of page 33 to find North and then line up the North end of your map so that it points the same way. Then work out your position.

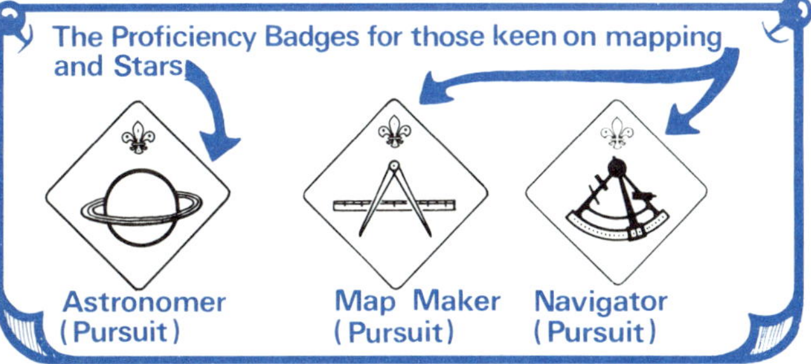

By compass

Look up the magnetic variation on the map – see the Orientation panel – say about 8°, and set your compass to this bearing where it says **read bearing here.** Now line up the compass needle and orienting arrow, making sure they are the right way round. Your compass now points to **Grid North.** If you now line up the vertical grid lines on the Ordnance Survey map with the long edge of the compass the map is **set.**

magnetic variation (or **declination**) which can be found in the Orienting panel on your O.S. map.

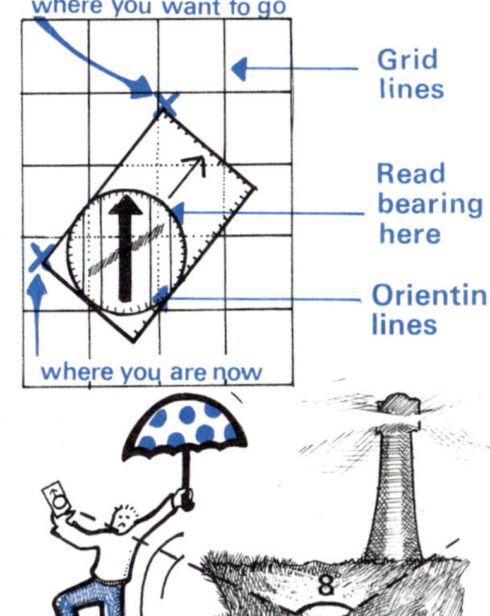

Finding a compass bearing.

Place the edge of your Silva Compass along the desired route you wish to travel. Rotate the dial until the compass orienting lines are parallel with the grid lines on your map, with the N (North) pointing to the top of your map.

Read the bearing where shown and by rotating the dial **anti-clockwise** ***add*** the

035°
N
043°
N

eg. bearing 035° + 8° (Mag. Var.) = 043°

If you forget this you can be 150 metres off course every kilometre.

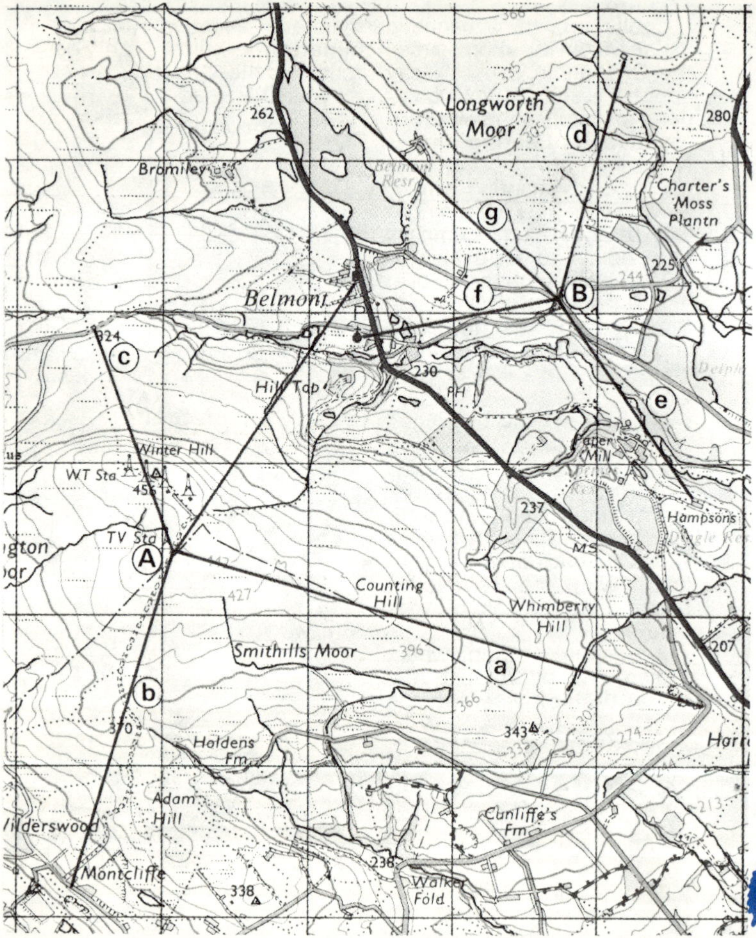

Practice in finding Bearings

Use the map extract opposite to practice finding bearings.

We'll do the first four bearings together then you try the second four bearings on your own, and **get your Patrol Leader to check them for you.**

Imagine you are standing at point **A**, the ITV television transmitter at Winter Hill in Lancashire.

We shall take the **Magnetic Variation** to be 8°.

Place your compass along the line drawn from **A** to **Belmont Church,** as instructed on page 35. You should find that the bearing is 035°. Add to this the magnetic variation of 8°, and this gives the corrected bearing of 043°.

Now check these yourself:

(a) From A to bend in road
Bearing = 105° + 8° = 113°

(b) From A to house at Montcliffe
Bearing = 197° + 8° = 205°

(c) From A to spot height 324
Bearing = 340° + 8° = 348°

Keeping the same magnetic variation, check the bearings of the four points centred on B.

(d) From B to hut on Longworth Moor
Bearing = ... + 8° = ...

(e) From B to Hampsons
Bearing = ... + 8° = ...

(f) From B to second church at Belmont
Bearing = ... + 8° ...

(g) From B to top of reservoir
Bearing = ... + 8° = ...

Map Scale and Distances

(1) Using string

Bend the string to follow the route you intend to take and then pull it taut and measure its length against the scale printed on the map. This will tell you how many miles (or kilometres) your route covers.

(2) Using a map measurer

A map measurer with a built in pocket compass can be obtained from Scout Shops Ltd. for under £4. You roll the wheel along your route and read off the distance on the dial.

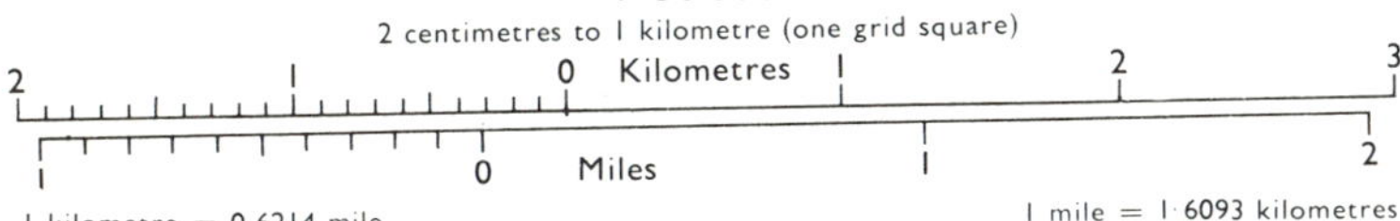

Patrol Leader—map reading cannot be learned just in the Troop Room. Give your Patrol as much practice out-of-doors as possible. How about a Patrol cycle expedition?

Do remember that **distances measured from a map will not make any allowance for the rise and fall of the ground.** There is a way of calculating your walking time as follows:

Naithsmiths' Rule for calculating route times:

Allow 4 kilometres per hour plus one additional hour for every 450 metres (1,500 feet) climbed.

If you are carrying a load, then the rule is:

Allow 3 kilometres per hour plus one additional hour for every 300 metres (1,000 feet) climbed.

Maps - keep them clean and dry on hikes in polythene bags.

Ordnance Survey maps are now published in Metric Editions. The First Series of the 1:50 000 maps is based on photographic enlargements of the old 1 inch = 1 mile series, but updated and with some new symbols. The Second Series will consist of completely redrawn maps with even more new symbols — the extract on page 38 is one of the new Second Series maps. The other 1:50 000 extracts in this book are First Series.

The 1:50 000 means that 1 unit (e.g. 1cm) on the map represents 50 000 units on the ground. This is called a Representative Fraction.

Conventional Signs

Conventional signs are best learned on a hike or cycle ride. These signs are changing on Ordnance Survey maps. Different signs for the same features appear on the **1 inch = 1 mile** maps, the **First Series 1:50 000** maps and the **Second Series 1:50 000** maps, but eventually the **Second Series** will become the standard maps. We show below one or two 'new' symbols and changed symbols used on the **Second Series 1:50 000** maps.

Hike Route

Plan a hike route using this map then work out the total distance travelled. See how many of the conventional signs you can recognise. **What information does this map not show you?** Discuss it with your Patrol Leader.

Beauty spot, place of historic interest, historic house, country park, ancient monument

View point

Parking

Information centre

Public telephone

Motoring organisation telephone

Public convenience (in rural areas)

Camp site

Heliport

Golf course or links

Windmill with or without sails

Chimney or tower

Caravan site

Picnic site

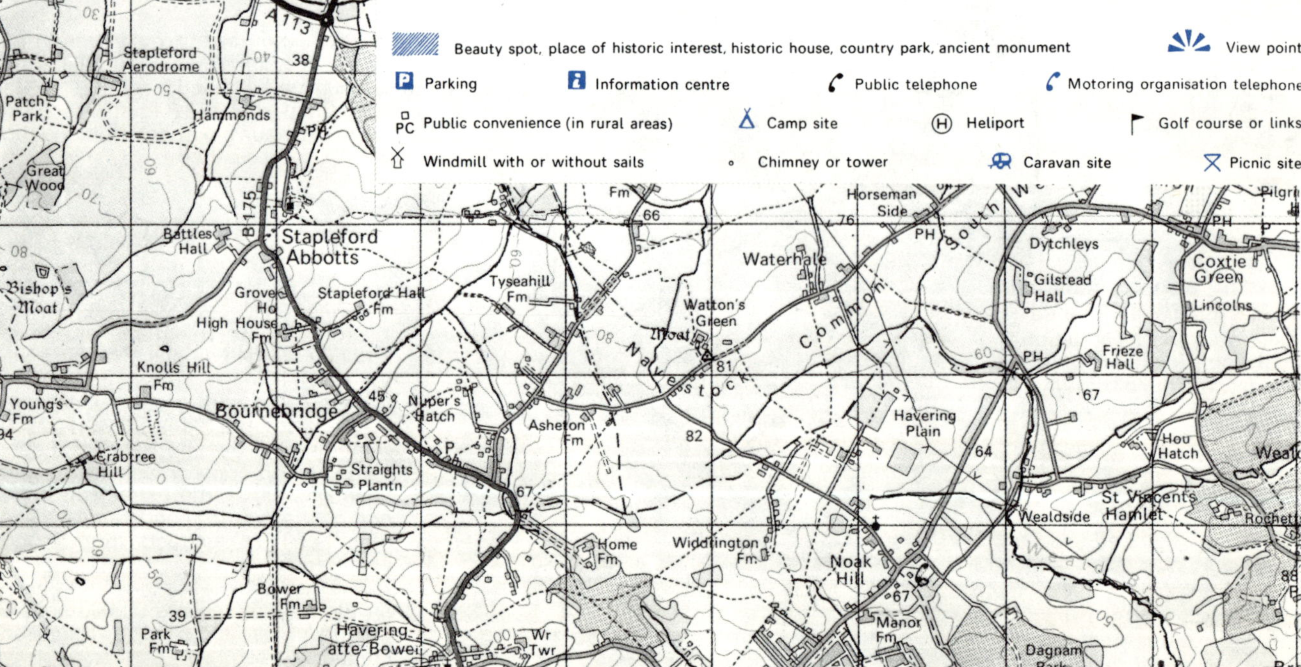

Getting About

(c) **Go on a 10 kilometre (6-mile) hike with a friend of your own age, and on return make a verbal report of a set objective achieved en route (eg. sketch or obtain specific knowledge about some place or person). This may be carried out at home or abroad.**

(d) **Demonstrate an understanding of the *Country* and *Highway Codes.***

Try to carry out this hike in an area that is not familiar to you, it's much more fun! Your companion does not have to be a Scout—he (*or even she*!) might join the Scouts (or Guides) if they enjoy themselves!

Remembering **a Scout is a brother to all Scouts**, if you do the expedition abroad you might try to team up with a Scout from that country.

Take with you:

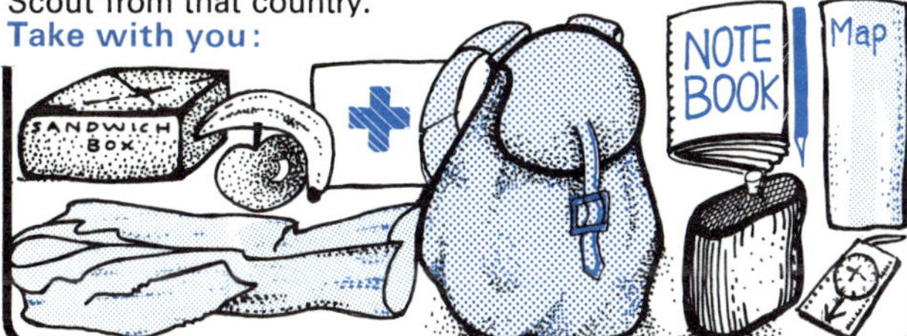

Leave a copy of your route and your estimated time of return with your Patrol Leader so that he can arrange help if anything goes wrong. If you don't do this nobody will know where to look. Also, don't wander off your route if you can help it.

Objectives

One objective of your journey should certainly be to put into practice all that you have learned during your Scout Standard, in particular map reading and the *Highway* and *Country Codes* (see next page).

Other objectives might be to photograph or tape record wild life, record an interview with a farmer, follow a river or canal or Roman Road or collect nature specimens. Try to keep off roads—use footpaths and bridle paths.

Keeping a notebook

You'll find it helpful to make notes on your journey to remind you of what you experienced when you give your report—of course if you have a cassette recorder or a polaroid camera, you could use that too.

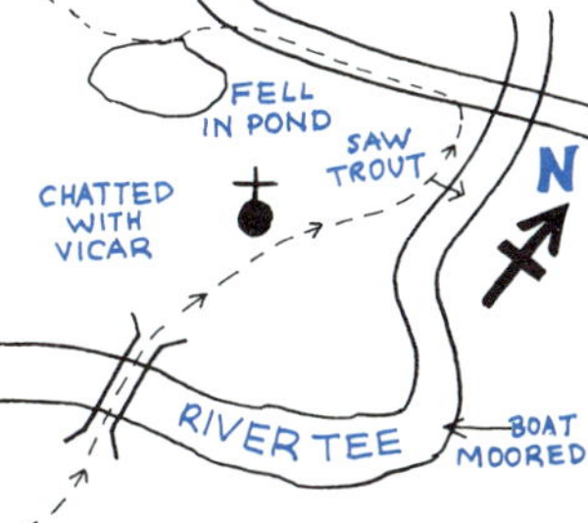

Make notes on

The weather—wind direction; did it stay that way or change; clouds; etc.

Farming—types of crop; arable or dairy farming?

Countryside — woodland; streams, lakes, rivers, fish?

Other things—are railways diesel or electric? What were fences and houses built from? What wild life did you see?

Make a sketch map of your route with notes of items of interest on it. Sketches or photos of what you saw will make it more interesting.

Your Patrol Leader might invite you to give your report to the Patrol, but he'll also be looking for evidence of enjoyment and that you did more than just walk!

In the sixth Scout Law, you promised to be **careful of possessions and property**, and one of the most important areas you can practice this is in the countryside.

Because of their high standards Scouts are one of the few groups of campers for whom farmers do not require a Public Health Licence to allow them to camp on their land. So help us to keep this privilege, and follow the *Country Code:*

- Guard against all risk of fire.
- Fasten all gates.
- Keep dogs under proper control.
- Keep to paths across farm land.
- Avoid damaging fences, hedges and walls.
- Leave no litter.
- Safeguard water supplies.
- Protect wild life, wild plants and trees.
- Go carefully on country roads.
- Respect the life of the countryside.

Scout's Special Supplement to the *Country Code:*

- Don't go on land with crops.
- Don't leave water taps dripping: water is precious to the farmer.
- Remove turf with care so it can be replaced.
- Only climb trees if you have permission.
- **Be sure to get permission before you get firewood,** and then be careful not to injure living trees or break down hedges or fences.
- Keep quiet after sunset, particularly near farmhouses—country people start work early and won't appreciate a disturbed night's sleep.
- Leave animals alone unless you are given permission to help with them.

There is no point in reprinting the *Highway Code* in this book—your Patrol Box will have an up-to-date copy in it. As a Scout loyal to the Queen, you should not only be concerned with obeying the Code, but in helping the police to make sure others do, too.

In some countries Scouts actually take over traffic control when called upon—but don't you try it!

Make sure your bicycle is in roadworthy condition—brakes, lights, steering, tyres, saddle height. Keep it maintained.

Help young children, the old and the blind to cross roads safely. Use **Zebra** and **Pelican** crossings properly.

Always wear a seat-belt in a car even if the driver doesn't. The front passenger seat is the most dangerous in an accident.

Always wear a crash-helmet when travelling on a motor-cycle or scooter.

Know what to do in the event of a road accident.

Cyclist (Interest)

Boatman

World Conservation (Collective)

Scouts doing the Sea Training Boatman Badge will need to know the water ***Rules of the Road*** **as well.**

THE COUNTRY CODE

THE HIGHWAY CODE

Getting About

(e) Find out about a foreign country, work out an interesting route to it, and tell your Patrol about the main things you would expect to find there.

The basic thing to remember about this requirement is that it is meant to be practical, not just extra Geography homework!

Read page 7 again, which shows you different ways of getting in touch with Scouts in other countries.

Here's one way of tackling the project:

World Friendship (Pursuit)

This badge links up with this test.

1 Choosing the country.

This will be limited by your sources of information, but you may have friends or relatives abroad or even be going abroad with the Troop, your parents or school, so that can help.

2 Sources of information.

Your own experience if you have been abroad; travel agents, public libraries, foreign visitors, magazines and films are other possibilities.

3 Limit your project.

You will find it more interesting if you specialise in certain aspects of the country—natural history, meals (make a typical meal for your Patrol); geography and places of interest; industry and Scouting.

4 Presenting your report.

A good report will be more than just a talk. Maps, photographs, wallcharts (**make them yourself**), meals, music, models, souvenirs—all of these will make it worthwhile.

This can be a nerve-racking experience if you've never given a report before, but your Patrol Leader will make sure that your Patrol carry out the Third Scout Law (considerate) and give you a fair hearing. It's better to prepare too much and not say it all than to prepare too little and woffle! Ten to 15 minutes is about right.

Scouting Skills

(a) **Explain how to use and care for a knife and axe. Use a knife to whittle a tent-peg (or other object) from a piece of wood, and an axe to prepare wood for a fire.**

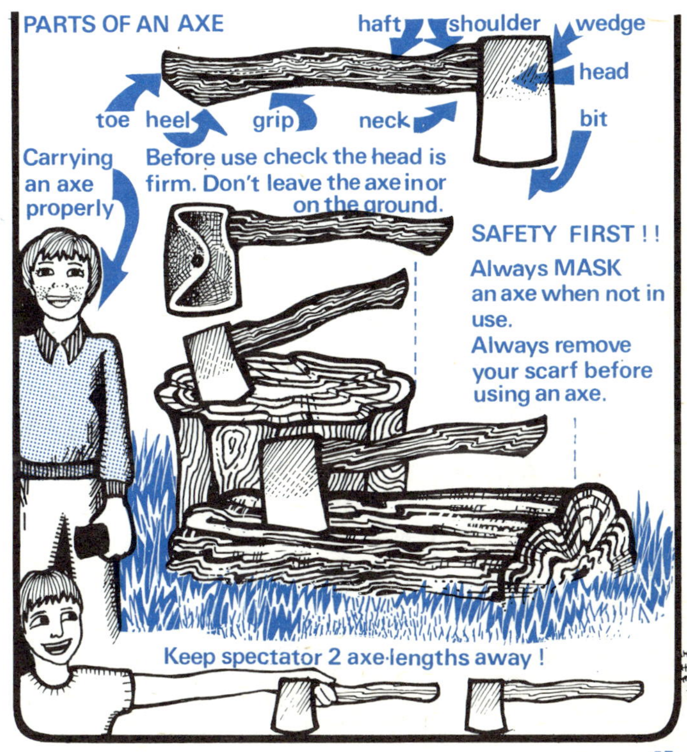

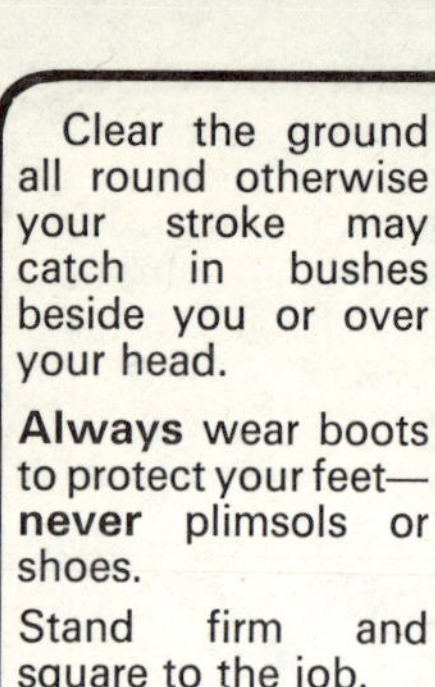

Clear the ground all round otherwise your stroke may catch in bushes beside you or over your head.

Always wear boots to protect your feet—**never** plimsols or shoes.

Stand firm and square to the job.

Always use a chopping block.

The part being cut must be resting on the block. Make sure the block is big enough.

A handsaw is useful.

Sit comfortably, resting your arms on your legs.

Things to carve.
Egg cup
Patrol totem

whittling
Always cut away from yourself.
Never stick or throw knives into the ground.

Never use an axe when you are tired.

Care
Keep axes and knives clean and sharp.
Occasionally rub wooden handles with linseed oil.

Bicycle oil.

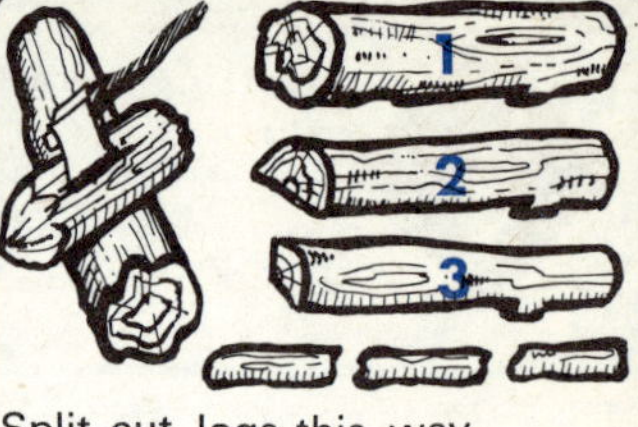

Split cut logs this way.

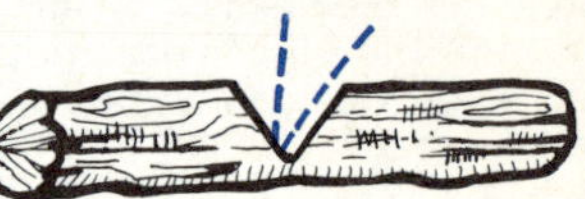

For heavier timber cut a large V but a saw is better than an axe.

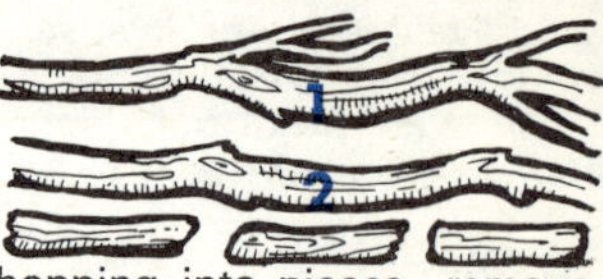

Chopping into pieces—remove side branches first.

If you enjoy whittling, here's a badge to try: Model maker (Interest)

Air Scouts make models in the Airman Badge.

Scouting Skills

(b) **Demonstrate any three knots, bends or hitches and two lashings useful in camp or on a boat.**

Reef

Use a reef knot for bandages – it lies flat

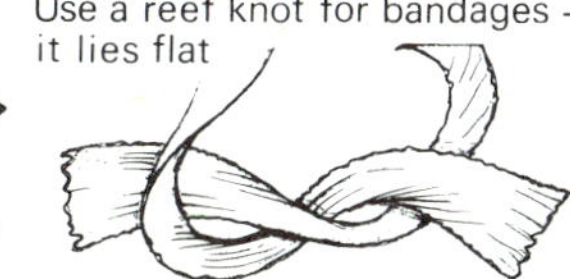

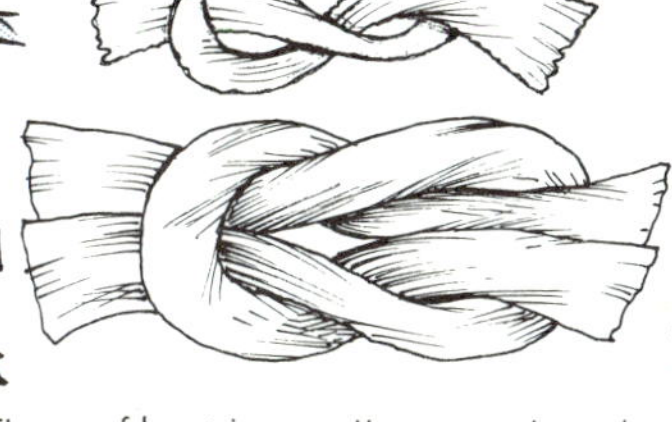

The reef knot is usually remembered by left over right, then right over left. It is used for joining ropes together.

Slip Reef

The slip reef is made in the same way, but instead of tucking an end through, you tuck a bight (loop) through. Used for fastening tent doors because it comes undone easily, by pulling the free end.

Round Turn and 2 Half-hitches

– useful for tying up a boat

Sheet-Bend

for joining ropes of unequal thickness.

Double Sheet-Bend

for joining ropes to rings or very unequal ropes together.

Clove Hitch

End of rope method

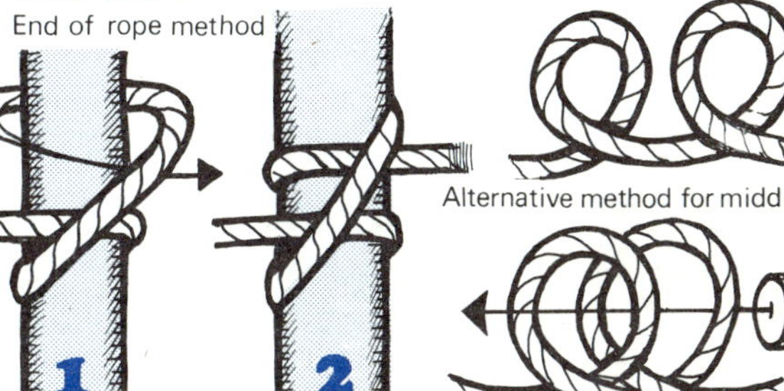

The Clove Hitch does not slip, is used to start and end lashings, but is unsuitable if the strain on each side is unequal.

Figure-of-Eight Knot

Used as a 'stopper' knot at the end of a rope. Useful if rope needs whipping. (see Advanced Scout Standard Book).

Your Patrol Leader will show you how to do these.
Other knots and/or lashings may be used.

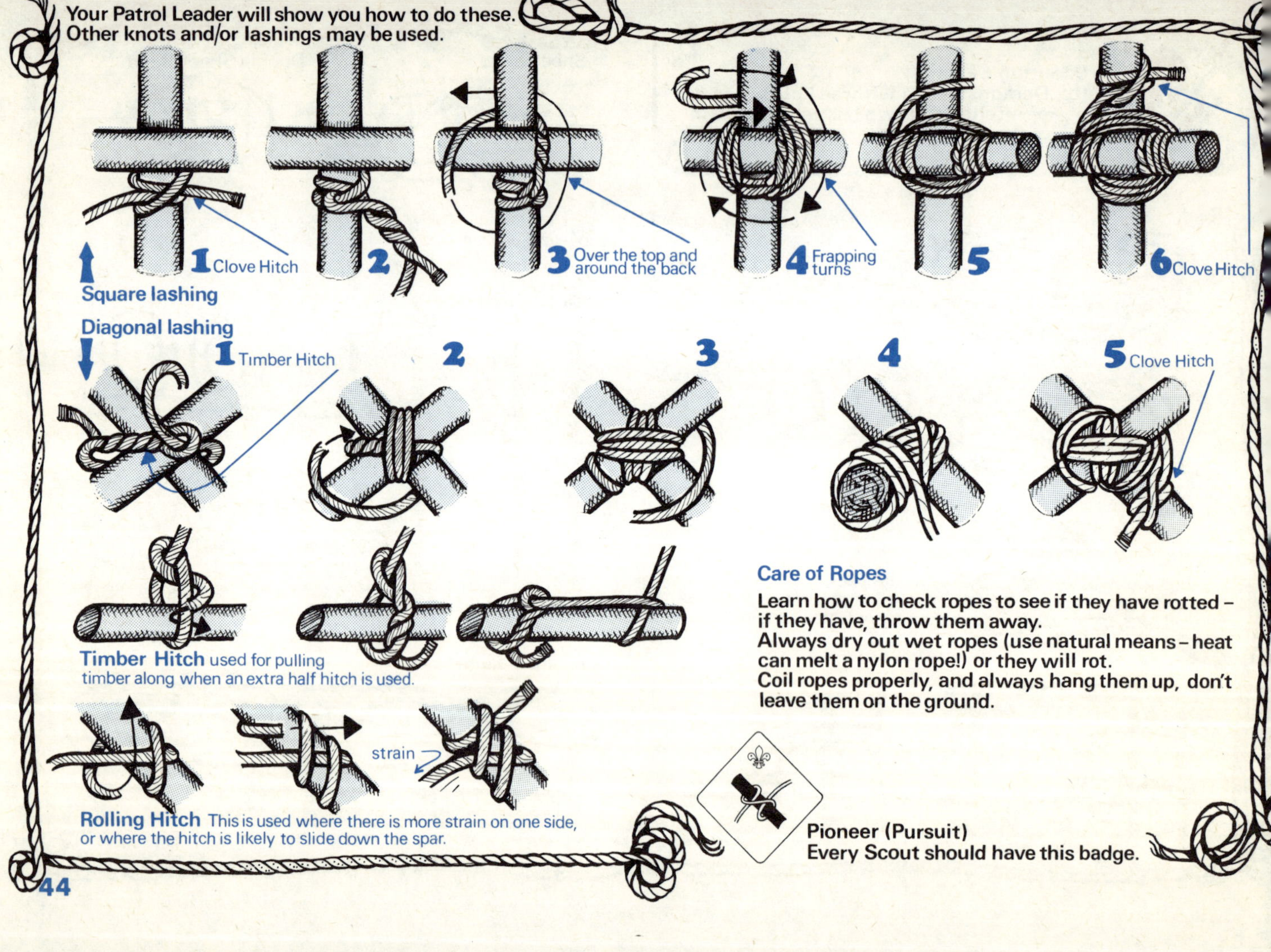

Timber Hitch used for pulling timber along when an extra half hitch is used.

Rolling Hitch This is used where there is more strain on one side, or where the hitch is likely to slide down the spar.

Care of Ropes

Learn how to check ropes to see if they have rotted – if they have, throw them away.
Always dry out wet ropes (use natural means – heat can melt a nylon rope!) or they will rot.
Coil ropes properly, and always hang them up, don't leave them on the ground.

Scouting Skills
(c) **Show a general knowledge and interest in weather conditions and signs and, where appropriate, relate these to your home area.**

Scouts going camping or hiking, and in particular climbing mountains or caving, Sea Scouts going sailing, especially at sea, and Air Scouts going flying or gliding, all need information about the weather. The purpose of this test is to enable you to anticipate changes in the weather so that, if you need to, you can seek safety in good time. On mountains a fine hot day can become a raging blizzard in five minutes, and if this is going to happen you want to know as soon as possible.

Obtaining Weather Forecasts

You can get hold of up-to-date forecasts in newspapers and on the radio and TV, but these will not necessarily be detailed enough for specific areas. You can get very local forecasts from airports, coastguards, certain mountain rescue posts, and by telephone.

Clouds

Learn to recognise cloud-types and the weather associated with them.

Wind

Estimating wind speeds is important to hikers and climbers because of the **wind-chill** factor. Greatly simplified, this means that if you subtract half of the **wind-speed** in mph. from the **temperature in degrees Celsius** (Centigrade) this is the **equivalent temperature** you are experiencing. If the wind is 30 mph. (strong breeze) and the temperature is 10 °C (50 °F), the conditions are similar to a temperature of —5 °C; in other words **below freezing point**! (The exact value is — 2 °C, but you can see it's close). So wind **even on warm days** can be dangerous. You'll learn about this in your **Advanced Scout Standard.**

Learn the Beaufort Wind Scale and how to work out wind speeds.

Weather signs and conditions

You will be expected to know what causes different weather conditions; some of the traditional ways of forecasting weather—granny's bunions or 'red sky at night . . .', and also the precautions to take.

1 Cirro-Cumulus mackerel sky **2** Cirrus mares tails **3** Cumulus fair weather **4** Cumulo-Nimbus thunder

Recommended reading
Ladybird Book of The Weather. Know the Weather in the *Know the Game* series.
The Weather Guide published by Hamlyn.

scale no:	mph	
0	less than 1	Smoke rises vertically.
1	1–3	Direction shown by smoke, not by vanes.
2	4–7	Wind felt on face, leaves rustle, vane moves.
3	8–12	Leaves and twigs in constant motion, light flag extended.
4	13-18	Dust and small paper raised, small branches move.
5	19-24	Small trees in leaf sway.
6	25-31	Large branches move, whistling in telegraph wires, umbrellas are difficult to control.
7	32-38	Whole trees move, inconvenience in walking against wind.
8	39-46	Twigs break off trees, walking is difficult.
9	47-54	Slight structural damage to buildings, branches break.
10	55-63	Trees uprooted, buildings sometimes blown down.

Beaufort Wind Scale (Goes up to scale no: 17)

Hobbies and interests

Demonstrate to your Patrol or Troop some skill or proficiency in a personal hobby or interest.

Examples: cycling, swimming, nature study, weather lore, aircraft recognition, stars, horse-riding, model making, basket work, stamp collecting, literature, drawing, decorating, radio construction, joinery.

These are examples only and other interests or pursuits may qualify.

Sorry, mate! Watching T.V. does not count!

Of course, records, films or tapes could depending on what they are, or if you made them yourself.

Pictured opposite are just some of the **Interest** range of Scout Proficiency Badges you could look through and try for, and perhaps gain at the same time. Then there are the **Pursuit Badges**, some of which we've already mentioned, but remember, **you can try hobbies or interests that are not listed as proficiency badges.** If you're interested in amateur dramatics, why not put on a show for your Patrol/Troop? If you're interested in writing, why not produce a Patrol magazine—then send a copy to Headquarters. You may get a mention in TAKE AIM—the Patrol Leaders' Supplement—in SCOUTING magazine! Does your Patrol Leader get it for your Patrol? **If not, sort him out**! Order it through your newsagent—it comes out monthly.

How about Karting? Parascending? Knitting! Collecting antiques (put Skip down!), signalling, cooking, there's lots of things you can do!

The only thing is you must **demonstrate** your interest, not just talk about it. Some hobbies may be difficult to demonstrate—space travel and rocket engines—and others—dancing (some Scouts aged 11-13 have won competitions in this!)—may require some courage!

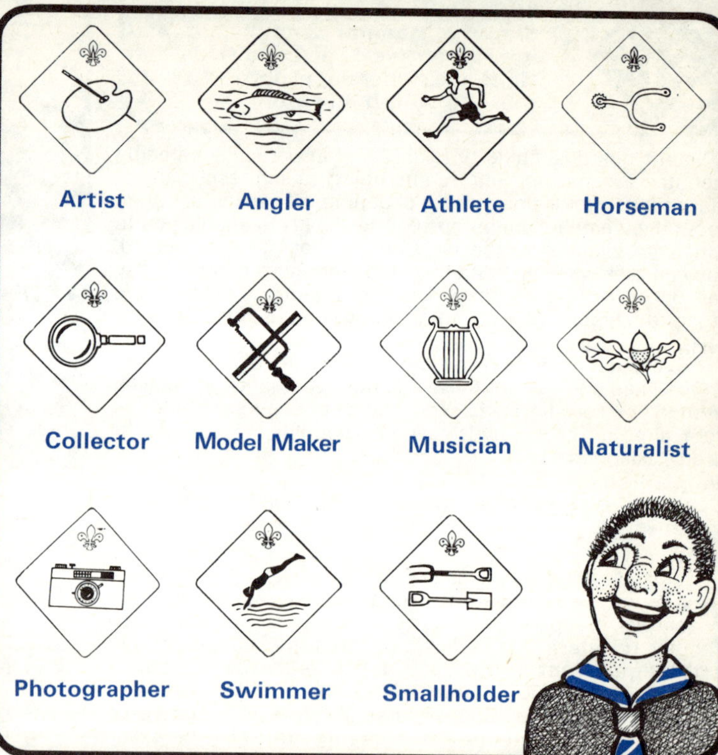

Patrol Leader—did you know that SCOUTING magazine supplies large wallcharts that will help you train the Scouts in your Patrol? An up-to-date list appears in each month's issue.

Promise and Law
Discuss with your Patrol Leader your progress in Scouting including living by the Promise and Law, and plan your future progress.

The Cornwell Scout Badge is an award presented to Scouts in respect of pre-eminently high character and devotion to duty, together with great courage, endurance or gallantry. It is granted only to Scouts under the age of 18 who have an outstanding record of service and efficiency.

Jack Cornwell

Jack Cornwell

On June 2nd. 1916, a Scout whose name has become a part of Scouting died in Grimsby Hospital—Jack Cornwell—he was 16 years old.

When he left school he became a van boy with a tea firm. When he was 15½ he joined the Royal Navy, and in July 1915 he entered the Boys' Training Establishment at the Royal Naval Barracks in Devonport. In May 1916 he was appointed to **H.M.S. Chester** and acted as **sight-setter** on his gun, a most difficult and responsible position. He would receive his instructions by earphones from an Officer higher up who could see the target, and set the dials which governed the aiming of the gun.

It was World War I, and on May 31st. 1916, H.M.S. Chester was sent into action—the Battle of Jutland. The Chester engaged in battle with three or four enemy light cruisers. A salvo at short range swept the Chester's decks—the concentrated fire of all the guns of one of the cruisers, and it brought disaster to Jack Cornwell's gun crew. Every man was dead, dying or wounded—only Jack remained at his post, but his face was white and drawn. A shell fragment had struck him near the heart. He was dying.

The battle raged on, but still he stood alone despite great pain, waiting steadfastly for orders in case he might be wanted. The battle ended, and he was carried below.

He was buried with full naval honours. A thousand Scouts attended his funeral and he was awarded the **Victoria Cross.** The highest award for valour in the Scout Movement—the **Bronze Cross**, was awarded to him and sent to his parents by B.-P.

He was an ordinary boy, full of jokes and plans, but he kept his Promise, **to do his duty to the King**, just as you have promised to do your duty to the Queen. Since his death the Cornwell Scout Badge (sometimes known as **the Scouts V.C.**) has been awarded in his memory.

All through this book we have mentioned the **Scout Promise and Law** to try to show that it is part of how we live, not just something we say. Jack Cornwell kept his Promise—**how have you kept yours?**

To help you find out, **we've left this part of the book for you to write**! The Law and Promise are written out for you. What we're inviting you to do is jot down what you've learned about them since you started the Scout Standard. Write what you've **done**, too!

The Scout Promise

The Scout Law

On my honour I promise that I will do my best –

To do my duty to God . . .	A Scout is to be trusted
. . . and to the Queen,	A Scout is loyal
To help other people	A Scout is friendly and considerate
And to keep the Scout Law	A Scout is a brother to all Scouts

A Scout makes good use of his time . . .	A Scout has courage in all difficulties
. . . and is careful of possessions and property	A Scout has respect for himself and for others.

Personal Progress

Proficiency Badges gained:	Camps attended, etc.

I gained my Scout Standard on ....

Future Plans: